OPPORTUNITIES

in

Teaching English to Speakers of Other Languages

REVISED EDITION

BLYTHE CAMENSON

Mc Graw Hill

New York Chicago San Francisco Lisbon London Madrid Mexico City
Milan New Delhi San Juan Seoul Singapore Sydney Toronto

Library of Congress Cataloging-in-Publication Data

Camenson, Blythe.
   Opportunities in teaching English to speakers of other languages /
Blythe Camenson. —Rev. ed.
        p.   cm.
      ISBN 0-07-147610-5 (acid-free paper)
        1. English language—Study and teaching—Foreign speakers—Vocational guidance.
2. English teachers—Employment—Foreign countries.   3. Americans—Employment—
Foreign countries.   I. Title.

   PE1128.A2C32   2007
   428.0023—dc22   2006028906

1 2 3 4 5 6 7 8 9 10 11 12 13 14 15 16 17 18 19   DOC/DOC   1 0 9 8 7

ISBN-13: 978-0-07-147610-2
ISBN-10:   0-07-147610-5

Interior design by Rattray Design

McGraw-Hill books are available at special quantity discounts to use as premiums and
sales promotions, or for use in corporate training programs. For more information, please
write to the Director of Special Sales, Professional Publishing, McGraw-Hill, Two Penn
Plaza, New York, NY 10121-2298. Or contact your local bookstore.

This book is printed on acid-free paper.

CONTENTS

Difference between ESL and EFL. Employment outlook. Job settings. What makes a good ESL/EFL teacher? What an ESL/EFL teacher does. Student profiles. At home or abroad? Advantages. Disadvantages.

ESL/EFL teacher training. The right qualifications. Requirements. How to choose wisely. Training required. What level do you want to teach? International teaching assistants. Picking your specialty. Learning the language. Volunteering. The cost of education. Ongoing professional development.

PREFACE

SINCE THE FIRST edition of this book was published in 1995, the world has become quite a cozy place. Thanks to the Internet and advanced telecommunications, business and culture have bled across international borders as never before. Language has followed. As *New York Times* columnist Thomas Friedman says, the world is flat. And English has become the common thread for millions of new members of the global community. The British Council estimates that 1.1 billion people are learning English either as a second language (every day for business or personal communication) or as a foreign language (for occasional conversation). By 2015, 2 billion people will be learning English, and another billion already will be speaking it.

In recognition of technology-driven language advancements, this second edition provides an extensive rundown of the sites that TESOL instructors are using to find jobs, stay current in the field, commiserate with colleagues, and expand their horizons. You'll also find updated coverage of salaries, working conditions, scams, and opportunities in the various countries seeking English-language teachers. Before you decide what sort of class setting to teach in, whether to stay in North America or go abroad, or even whether teaching English to non-native speakers is the field for you, read up on the experiences of those who have gone before you and the strategies for smoothing out the inevitable bumps in the road that come with living in a foreign country. If you're like many TESOL-ers, you'll find that the job is both challenging and more rewarding than you ever imagined, and you'll come away as influenced by the local culture as your students are by yours.

Teaching has never been one of the best-paying professions, but for TESOL instructors the dividends are undoubtedly rich: the chance to explore other countries as a native instead of a tourist, lifelong friends, favorable exchange rates, and knowledge from living abroad that can pay off handsomely down the road with North American employers. Far from becoming a monolingual society of English speakers, the world is moving toward a multilingual model where Chinese, Spanish, Arabic, Hindi, and other languages will have a prominent place in the cultural exchange. In that setup, English will be not so much a force for homogenization as a conduit for the transmission of ideas and traditions from all over the world directly into the mainstream. With your help, millions more people will be able to tap into it in the years to come.

Acknowledgments

I WOULD LIKE to thank all the professional associations and agencies involved in international education and their staff members, too numerous to mention here, who generously provided information and answered all my questions.

A special thanks to Sharon Bolton, TESOL's Coordinator of Continuing Education, who answered all my questions—twice.

I would also like to thank Brad Crawford for his assistance in preparing this edition.

Acronyms

Professionals in the world of TESOL use a variety of acronyms to simplify program names. Newcomers to the field might find the array confusing because many of the acronyms are used interchangeably. Here are the acronyms—and what they stand for—that are used in this book.

CALL—Computer-Assisted Language Learning

EAP—English for Academic Purposes

EFL—English as a Foreign Language refers to programs where students learn English for business or tourism or to complete an academic language requirement at an institution in their own country.

ESL—English as a Second Language refers to programs where students live and work among native speakers but do not speak English as a first language. Students can be immigrants or refugees with a real need to learn English to communicate, work, and study.

ESOL—English to Speakers of Other Languages refers to English programs in elementary and secondary schools in the United States. Students are immigrants or refugees, and English is not their first language.

ESP—English for Specific Purposes

IATEFL—International Association of Teachers of English as a Foreign Language is a UK-based association representing teachers of English as a foreign or second language.

INS—Immigration and Naturalization Service

ITA—International Teaching Assistant

LEP—Limited English Proficiency

TESL/TEFL—Teaching English as a Second Language or Foreign Language refers to ESL/EFL programs in the United Kingdom or in other English-speaking countries outside the United States. The terms also refer to the degree or certificate teachers obtain in countries other than the United States.

TESOL—Teaching English to Speakers of Other Languages refers to the degree a person earns to become a teacher in the field in the United States. For example, a person can study for a master's degree or a certificate in TESOL. Teachers of English to Speakers of Other Languages is also the name of the professional association with nearly 13,500 ESL/EFL teachers, program administrators, curriculum developers, materials writers, researchers, and teacher trainers as members. TESOL promotes scholarship, disseminates information, and strengthens instruction and research. TESOL's mission is to foster effective teaching and learning of English around the world while respecting individuals' language rights.

TOEFL—The Test of English as a Foreign Language (pronounced TOE-ful) is administered around the world to international students applying to U.S. universities. The results are used by university admissions officials to determine applicants' English-language capabilities and eligibility for study.

1

WHAT IS TESOL?

TRAINED AND EXPERIENCED teachers who have made teaching English as a second or foreign language (ESL/EFL) a long-term career work in the profession known as TESOL, which stands for teachers of English to speakers of other languages. They have studied in accredited programs, working toward certification with bachelor's and master's degrees. They are familiar with up-to-date ESL/EFL teaching methodology and classroom materials, have acquired an awareness of other cultures, and are sensitive to their differences.

The mission of TESOL, the professional organization and backbone of the field, is to "ensure excellence in English language teaching to speakers of other languages." With a membership of nearly 13,500, which includes teachers, teachers-in-training (and their trainers), administrators, curriculum developers, researchers, and materials writers in more than 140 countries, the profession continues to grow strong.

Difference Between ESL and EFL

ESL stands for English as a second language and TESL for teaching English as a second language. Students in these programs are living in an environment where English is not their first language. They might be immigrants or refugees in an English-speaking country and need to learn the language to cope with day-to-day life.

EFL stands for English as a foreign language and TEFL for teaching English as a foreign language. Students in these programs may live in a country where their own language is the primary tongue; they may need to learn English for academic study, in preparation for travel to an English-speaking country, or for business purposes.

For some professionals the terminology might be helpful in defining the students, but, in essence, it doesn't reflect any critical differences in teaching methods or approach. Others feel that there are differences—in approach and cultural content of materials—and that the ESL versus EFL terminology should reflect those differences.

A few recognized differences between the disciplines:

- EFL learners generally spend fewer hours per week studying English than their ESL counterparts in settings within English-speaking countries.
- EFL learners have little exposure to English outside the classroom and also have little need or opportunity to practice their newly acquired language skills.
- A classroom of EFL learners has a common native-language background. ESL classes generally consist of students from a variety of countries.

For the purpose of this book, the term ESL/EFL is used throughout, except when specifically referring to domestic versus overseas teaching situations.

Employment Outlook

An estimated one billion people around the world are currently learning English. They choose to learn English for any number of reasons: to attend colleges and universities in English-speaking countries, to have better business communications, to enhance their employability, to facilitate government relations, to create a more rewarding travel experience, or, for many, to be able to communicate day to day in the English-speaking country in which they reside.

A 2005 U.S. Department of Education report noted that between 1979 and 2003 the number of U.S. schoolchildren (ages five to seventeen) who spoke a language other than English at home grew from 3.8 million to 9.9 million. Another U.S. Department of Education report, from 2006, says that 43.8 percent of U.S. adults enrolled in adult education programs in 2003–2004 were enrolled in ESL classes.

These are low estimates. It is, of course, impossible to document all the potential language learners who didn't participate in the surveys and those who aren't participating in any program. One TESOL professional who spent several years teaching ESL in Boston remembers waiting lists of up to four hundred for a single program. It would be safe to say that most programs have similar waiting lists. And many potential students, perhaps feeling that their names will never be called, choose not to be put on waiting lists.

What does all this mean? The number of people in the United States desiring ESL instruction is on the rise. It can also be assumed that the need for English language instruction is increasing worldwide. (There's an extensive list of job-hunting resources in Appendix A.) As the public school system, government agencies, and private enterprise continue to work toward filling the demand, opportunities for ESL/EFL teachers will continue to grow.

In fact, the field of teaching English as a second or foreign language (TESL/TEFL) has grown enormously over the past two decades. At one time, it was believed that the only qualification necessary to teach English to non-native speakers was to be a native speaker. But these days that school of thought has almost vanished. Before the TESOL profession firmly established itself as an important and valid discipline, an individual could go overseas and find teaching work along the way to cover travel and living expenses. Although such tutoring and part-time teaching situations still exist in a few locations, they are quickly shrinking, replaced with quality programs touting qualified and experienced ESL/EFL teachers.

Job Settings

As the need for English-language instruction increases, so does the variety of locations in which ESL/EFL teachers can work. Teachers of English as a second language are finding that their skills are more and more in demand, and the better their qualifications, the better their employment outlook is.

Teachers of English as a second language generally work with students from varied cultural and language backgrounds. They teach students who have come to study, work, or live in the United States or Canada. They teach day and evening classes in adult-education programs, work as certified teachers in the public school systems at both the elementary and secondary levels, or instruct incoming international students at university-based language centers. They also find work in private language schools teaching students from around the world.

Areas of the country that have been most affected by refugees or immigration offer the greatest opportunities for employment. Major cities such as San Diego, Los Angeles, San Francisco, and Seattle on the West Coast and Miami, Washington, DC, Baltimore, New York, and Boston on the East Coast generally have more private and government-funded language instruction programs than less-populated locations. However, most universities across the United States have an international student population, from Asia or the Middle East, for example, and require teachers to staff their language centers.

Teachers of English as a foreign language work overseas in international schools, for overseas companies or private companies with overseas concerns, for the Peace Corps, or centers for English language instruction based around the world. An extensive list of job contacts for a variety of countries can be found in Appendix B.

ESL/EFL teachers can find employment almost anywhere, although the largest concentration of jobs appears to be in the United States; in Middle Eastern countries such as Saudi Arabia; in the Far East in countries such as Japan, China (including Hong Kong), and South Korea; in Turkey and Poland; in Egypt and Morocco; and throughout Central and South America.

Teaching environments and working conditions can vary widely. ESL/EFL teachers could find themselves working in a modern classroom outfitted with state-of-the-art equipment and teaching aids—computers, DVDs, and videos—or in a more primitive setting with tin-roofed buildings and outdated materials, if any at all. There could be chalkboards but no chalk or computers but only intermittent electricity. There are numerous possibilities, and you should take them all into account when deciding the conditions under which you would be most comfortable working.

What Makes a Good ESL/EFL Teacher?

Teaching English as a second or foreign language is not the same as teaching it as a first language. There is a foundation of knowledge and methodology for the first two fields of study that include linguistics, second language acquisition, education practices, sociology, anthropology, psychology, testing and measurement, and other related subjects.

In addition to strong foundations in these areas, ESL/EFL teachers must have a special talent; they carry weighty responsibilities. How they present their subject will affect their students' attitudes toward language learning, the English language in particular, as well as the teachers' countries and those cultures.

ESL/EFL teachers need to possess the same qualities that any teachers do: intelligence, patience, and creativity. They also have to have an understanding of the nature of language in general and how people learn languages. They must have cross-cultural knowledge and experience and be sensitive to individual differences among students. And in certain settings, they must also have knowledge of other areas related to international student affairs such as immigration and visa policies.

These additional qualities are vital to a successful career as a teacher of English as a second or foreign language:

- Experience traveling or living in international settings
- Enthusiasm for the subject matter
- Independence

- A sincere appreciation of people from different cultures
- Ability to work as part of a team
- Tolerance
- Flexibility
- Maturity
- Communication skills

A successful ESL/EFL teacher also maintains an interest in continuing professional development and helps to encourage the same interest in those he or she supervises, including other teachers and staff members.

Does a successful ESL/EFL teacher need to be a native speaker of English? Although a small contingent might argue for that requirement, most feel that it is an elitist attitude that should have no place in the field of TESOL. Why should every non-English-speaking country in the world have to depend on native English-speaking teachers for its ESOL instruction? French teachers, for example, with a solid command of the English language and professional qualifications from a recognized TESOL program are ultimately better equipped to help students in their own country understand the process of learning English. They would be more aware of the nuances, the specific French-to-English problems their students would have, than would a native English speaker.

But what if they are tempted to speak French in the classroom to help a student over a rough spot, when the method of instruction should be English to English? Again, this point is debatable. It is generally agreed that English should be the language of instruction in an ESOL classroom, but most don't see the harm—in fact, they can see the benefit—of an occasional translation to clear up points of confusion for students. Why waste precious classroom time when a quick aside will allow everyone to move on?

What an ESL/EFL Teacher Does

Many people not yet in the profession believe that because they can speak English they should be able to teach it. As mentioned earlier, some people without formal training are able to find employment, and often travelers wanting to earn extra money to help pay for their trips find work tutoring or providing practice in conversation skills. However, as the number of professionally trained teachers increases, opportunities for unqualified teachers decrease.

Professional ESL/EFL teachers go through a variety of training programs (see Chapter 2) studying methodology, second language acquisition, curriculum design, research methods, and basic language skills. They might also add particular specializations to their program such as computer-assisted language learning (CALL) or the use of video and digital media in the classroom.

ESL/EFL teachers instruct students in basic English language skills: reading, writing, listening, and conversation. Like any teachers, they are responsible for designing lesson plans and for administering and grading tests. They might also help develop the teaching program that will best meet their particular students' needs, such as writing materials to be used in the classroom.

Student Profiles

The students ESL/EFL teachers instruct could be primary or secondary school pupils, university students, or adults. In the United States and Canada, teachers work with refugees, immigrants, and short-term visitors such as businesspeople, tourists, and university students.

The language learners ESL/EFL teachers encounter overseas are generally residents of the country in which they are living and working. Students could be individuals or groups involved in private business or employees of the host country's government. They could be university students studying a program in English in their own country or native children attending local private schools. In addition, students could come from a variety of countries, such as the children of diplomats or international businesspeople.

Although personality is a very individual entity and no generalizations can be made about groups of people or the countries from which they come, it appears to be a safe assessment to say that most students of English as a second or foreign language are enthusiastic about learning the English language and becoming more intimate with the cultures it represents.

At Home or Abroad?

Among all the other decisions future ESL/EFL teachers have to make, from training programs to individual specializations, one of the most important is that of job setting. Will you stay in your home country or venture abroad?

Although teaching overseas is not a requirement for a successful career, the experience does greatly enhance one's employability and chances for advancement. Needless to say, the opportunity to travel overseas and get to know different countries in depth is one of the main reasons so many people are attracted to the profession.

Advantages

Most ESL/EFL teachers enjoy many of the same benefits as teachers of any subject—shorter working days and long summer vacations, for example. But for most ESL/EFL teachers, the main pleasure of the profession is not just the opportunity to travel but the chance to live for long periods of time in a variety of foreign countries. Those who opt to stay in the United States or Canada still enjoy a sort of vicarious travel by working with students from different countries.

And for most teachers, the ultimate reward comes from the students themselves. This is what three ESL/EFL teachers have to say on the subject:

> I helped prepare a Yemeni student for postgraduate study in Britain. I gave him extra tutoring in EFL and linguistics. Not only did he pass the program, he was the number one student. It was very gratifying.

> Rewarding moments for me were when the first group of students I had taught graduated, and years later, when several students came back to see me to tell me how much I had helped them.

> I still get letters from former students. I know in part that they want to practice their writing skills, but it feels wonderful to hear from them and see how they've improved.

Salaries and benefits are also pluses, but they vary from region to region and employer to employer. ESL pay scales in the United States and Canada are usually competitive with other teachers' salaries. In general, jobs overseas in areas that offer more "hardship" for Americans, such as the Middle East, pay higher wages and provide more special allowances. In such a setting you would probably receive free housing and furniture, free travel, free medical care, and a bonus at the end of your contract.

In poorer countries or in countries where the lifestyle is more compatible with what Americans or Canadians are used to, salaries are generally lower. However, when you work overseas and if you meet certain requirements, such as the length of time spent out of the United States or Canada, you will not be required to pay U.S. or Canadian income tax, only local taxes. The financial rewards of the profession are discussed in more detail in Chapter 4.

Finally, some U.S.-based TESL situations offer the bonus of job security. In most states, ESL teachers working within the public school system are protected by tenure laws stating that a teacher cannot be fired without good cause. While incompetence is still a basis for dismissal, a personality conflict with the principal is not.

Disadvantages

Most satisfied TESOLers will tell you that the advantages far outweigh the disadvantages. But still, those considering a career in this field should consider the disadvantages of teaching work in general. (Disadvantages of working abroad are discussed in Chapter 7.)

• **Low pay.** In spite of the lucrative benefit packages and earnings and saving potential afforded to ESL/EFL teachers in some overseas locations (discussed in Chapter 4), most teachers recognize that the salary level is far below that of other professionals such as doctors, attorneys, and engineers.

• **Stress.** How each teacher responds to stressful situations is a matter of individual temperament, but there are certain factors in the teaching profession that can lead to stress. Some of these include handling discipline problems in the classroom; meeting a new class for the first time; overcrowded classrooms; deadlines for grading papers or handing in exam scores; and inadequate materials or facilities.

As in any profession, stress can be generated by strained relations with coworkers, work assignments outside your usual scope of duties, and occasional boredom with the subject matter.

Stress can also be brought about by change, and for ESL/EFL teachers who travel abroad, the adjustment period to a new culture and new ways of doing things can create new levels of anxiety and tension. These levels usually decrease once the settling-in period is over, although they might escalate again upon departure. (See Chapter 8 for a more detailed discussion.)

Program administrators often suffer greater stress than do classroom teachers. The article "Too Busy to Care Anymore: Burnout and the ESL Program Administrator" by Claire Monro, published in *TESOL Matters,* sums up the situation:

> Job-related factors can cause burnout in vulnerable ESL administrators. Foremost among these is the nature of the ESL student population. These students require more attention than native English speakers. Unfamiliar with cultural and linguistic matters both on campus and in the larger community, they often depend on empathetic ESL faculty for help. If the administrator is available more than others in the program, that person may be the one to whom students come most frequently. . . . Another possible stressor is the onus of being the unofficial spokesperson and link between ESL students and the rest of the school.

But dedicated teachers learn to cope with the stress and other disadvantages or don't even regard them as such. One educational association has summed up the positives and negatives this way:

> Teachers do not make much money, but their jobs are usually stable and secure. Teachers spend long hours outside the classroom making preparations . . . working with faculty committees . . . ; but these undertakings contribute to the teachers' effectiveness in

the classroom and help them to become valued and responsible citizens of the community. Teachers live in a goldfish bowl of community attention and gossip, but they have many pleasant social contacts . . . . Teaching is monotonous work for some, but for others, it is highly individual, creative, and responsible. Teaching is hard work, but it is work that makes a difference in the lives of [students] and ultimately in the future of the nation.

2

TEACHING THE TEACHER

THERE IS A wide variety of employment opportunities for teachers of ESL/EFL, but where you will be able to work and, to some extent, the salary you earn will be determined by your qualifications. While many people with no qualifications other than being a native English speaker report finding teaching or tutoring positions, those jobs are quickly disappearing.

ESL/EFL Teacher Training

As the profession grows—as it has continued to do in the last forty or so years—and more and more teachers graduate from accredited training programs, ESL/EFL jobs will become more competitive and will more likely go first to qualified and experienced teachers. And the more qualifications and experience you have, the better the job setting, pay scale, and benefits.

But not only does training increase your employment chances, it can help enhance your sense of confidence when facing a classroom of eager language learners. Even a short-term course can provide you with the basic ESL/EFL teaching methodologies and introduce you to the latest materials.

The Right Qualifications

When you are deciding on how much training you will pursue, it is important to take into account the level at which you plan to teach. Classroom teachers working within U.S. school systems, for example, need at least a B.A.; overseas university language center instructors are expected, for the most part, to have earned a master's degree. In Canada teacher requirements vary by province and territory. Typically a university degree is needed with some specific study in teacher education.

ESL/EFL teachers, like all teachers, must be familiar with up-to-date teaching materials, classroom management methods, teaching methodology, lesson planning, and student evaluations. They also must be familiar with areas particular to ESL/EFL, including the following:

- Specific ESL/EFL materials, course design, and teaching methods
- The nature of language in general
- The nature of the English language in particular (phonology, lexicon, syntax, and pragmatics)
- The nature of second language acquisition
- The interaction of culture and language

ESL/EFL professionals are also expected to demonstrate certain specialized skills they can develop through experience as well as training. This can cover various interest areas such as computer-assisted language learning or the use of video and digital media in the classroom. It can expand to more administrative duties including curriculum development, course coordination, supervision of other teachers, and teacher training.

Requirements

Today there are certain educational requirements that you'll need to become a teacher of a second or foreign language.

Bachelor's Degree

A bachelor's degree is considered the basic requirement for employment. If the candidate expects to earn a master's degree, it is not necessary for the B.A. to be in TESOL. An undergraduate could major in English or foreign languages or international relations. But if the B.A. is to be the terminal degree, the program should cover courses such as the grammatical, phonological, and semantic systems of the English language; methodology and second-language assessment; the study of another language and its cultural system; and teaching practice.

State Teacher's Certification

Certification is required in most states for teaching ESL at the elementary and secondary levels in U.S. public schools. Contact your state board of education to learn what the certification requirements are. University teacher training programs will offer these required courses. A list of state certification/endorsement licensing requirements is provided in TESOL's *Directory of Teacher Education Programs in TESOL in the United States and Canada.*

U.S. Certification

After a student earns a bachelor's degree, he or she can acquire an ESL certificate, which is offered by many universities with teacher training programs, with another eighteen to twenty-four graduate credits. The U.S. certificate is considered adequate for many jobs in private language schools overseas and in some private language schools in the United States.

Canadian Certification

In the Canadian educational system, teaching requirements vary by province and territory. This means that there are no consistent requirements for ESL teachers within Canada. Rather, employers set their own standards for education and certification. A number of opportunities, however, call for teachers with a four-year degree and accreditation from one of two prominent organizations: Alberta Teachers of English as a Second Language (www.atesl.ca) or TESL Canada (www.tesl.ca).

UK Certification

These days, many North American as well as British teachers are earning TEFL certificates in the United Kingdom. The Cambridge certificate in English-language teaching to adults and the Trinity College London certificate in teaching English to speakers of other languages are two certificates that can open doors in the world of TESOL. Teachers earn these certificates in short-term intensive programs throughout the United Kingdom. Appendix C includes a short selection of these programs. Contact the program of your choice for applications, deadlines, requirements, and costs.

Master's Degree

A master's degree, in addition to a theoretical background, will prepare you in classroom teaching methods, curriculum development, and materials writing and offer an overview of program coordination. With a master's degree you will be qualified to teach in most settings in North America and abroad.

There are a variety of names for the different master's degrees, including M.A. in TESOL, M.Ed. in TESOL, M.A. in applied linguistics, M.A.T. in TESOL, or an M.A. in English with an emphasis in TESOL. An employer might specify one particular degree when advertising a position but is usually willing to consider any of the variations.

Ph.D. Degree

Those wishing to advance academically and become involved in language research, writing for professional publications, or teaching future ESL/EFL teachers at the master's level will need to pursue a Ph.D. degree.

TESOL's *Directory of Teacher Education Programs in TESOL in the United States and Canada* lists universities offering certificate, master's, and Ph.D. programs in TESOL. Write to TESOL, 700 South Washington Street, Suite 200, Alexandria, Virginia 22314 or visit www.tesol.org.

How to Choose Wisely

It is a good idea to compare programs for master's degrees before making your final choice. Some are more theoretical, some are more practical, some concentrate more on international issues than domestic, and vice versa—they all have different focuses.

There are general rankings available to help you compare graduate programs in education. *U.S. News & World Report* offers an annual guide to America's best graduate schools. Many of the rankings are available on the magazine's website at www.usnews.com. A good place to start exploring Canadian programs is the Association of Universities and Colleges of Canada (www.aucc.ca). The group's website includes a searchable database of programs. Once you've narrowed it down to one or two schools, it's a good idea to go for a campus visit. Talk to current students and faculty about the curriculum, career placement, and general environment. Be sure to ask where recent graduates are working. Find out about costs and whether teaching assistant positions are available to help defray those expenses. Many schools offer teaching assistants free or reduced tuition, as well as a modest salary.

According to the Center for National Education Statistics, part of the U.S. Department of Education, education is one of the most popular fields of study at the master's degree level. In the 2002–2003 school year, 147,000 master's degrees were conferred in education. Of course, the number of students pursuing a specialty in TESOL was much lower, though there is no exact figure.

Before making a serious commitment in terms of the number of years of training you will pursue, you can follow a few other options first to get a feel for the profession.

- Volunteer your time and take advantage of any of the in-house training the organization might offer.
- Enroll in a short-term intensive training program (several are listed in Appendix C) and work toward a certificate.

• After finishing your bachelor's degree, spend a year or two working in the field before going on for a master's program. (This tactic also helps beef up your résumé with valuable professional experience.)

Whatever you choose to do, it is best to start out with a plan. If you ask a handful of longtime ESL/EFL teachers how they got started, you might hear a string of similar and somewhat surprising answers:

"I fell into it; it wasn't something I had originally planned."

"I started off volunteering while I was pursuing another profession. I ended up staying in ESL."

"I did some tutoring when I was traveling in Europe, and one thing led to another. I went back later to get my master's degree."

"I took a summer job at a U.S. language institute; it helped me to get a teaching job overseas, and that job led to another job."

"I don't have any TEFL qualifications. My master's degree is in English literature, but I was hired anyway. Now, after ten years' overseas experience, I can work almost anywhere."

"My bachelor's is in French. While I was studying in Paris eight years ago, I met an EFL teacher at a language school there. There was an unexpected opening, and I just fell into it."

So many people who began teaching ESL/EFL twenty or more years ago will probably have responses similar to these teachers', but times have changed. These days, to land the plum jobs, teachers plan their programs very carefully. They choose courses that will meet their own needs and interests while also considering the needs and requirements of future employers.

Training Required

In 2003 TESOL released a position statement on "Teacher Quality in the Field of Teaching English to Speakers of Other Languages." It asserts that students in EFL or ESL settings have the right to a fully trained teacher—learning from a native English speaker just isn't enough to guarantee success in the classroom. The statement outlines the skills required for a teacher. Here are some of the necessary skills as outlined in the statement:

- A high level of written and oral proficiency in the English language
- Teaching competency
- An awareness of current trends and research in second-language acquisition and such related topics as linguistics
- Necessary degrees, certifications, and so forth, for the particular school and/or country
- Ongoing professional development

These are good points for prospective ESL/EFL teachers to keep in mind as they pursue training. While some native speakers land jobs overseas with no specialized training, it's not the best path to take. Being well trained opens up more job opportunities and gives language students the benefits of proven teaching methods.

What Level Do You Want to Teach?

With the above information in mind, there are a few other considerations to take into account when planning your TESOL preparation program. The various settings in which teachers can work require, to some extent, different preparation and qualifications. An ESL/EFL teacher interested in secondary education, for example, would need to qualify for a state teacher's certificate, while someone interested in teaching at the university level would not.

The level you choose will also reflect your interests. Are you more comfortable with adults, or do you enjoy working with children? Would you prefer an academic setting or a business environment? Your interests and the amount of time you are willing to commit to training will ultimately determine the level you will teach.

International Teaching Assistants

For those not interested in completing a full course toward a degree, work is available, particularly overseas, for international teaching assistants (ITAs). Often ITAs are natives of the country in which the instruction is taking place.

An international teaching assistant interest group within TESOL addresses all research, teaching, and administrative issues related to the preparation of international teaching assistants for instructional duties in university classrooms. Its purpose is to promote the sharing of expertise among ITAs, to foster research into classroom communication, and to encourage scholarship. A number of universities offer ITA training programs. Contact TESOL for more information.

Picking Your Specialty

In addition to deciding the age and proficiency level of students with whom you prefer to work, you can focus your training on a particular specialization. While it is important for you as an ESL/EFL teacher to be a generalist, to have a solid background in every aspect of the field, it can be helpful to your career to have more intensive training and experience in one or more particular areas.

What follows here is a list of the twenty-two interest sections TESOL recognizes as concerns within the TESOL profession. These sections provide a focus for individual members' specializations. Members of TESOL are each encouraged to join at least one interest section. They are:

- Adult education
- Applied linguistics
- Bilingual education
- Computer-assisted language learning
- Elementary education
- English as a foreign language
- English for specific purposes
- Higher education
- Intensive English programs
- Intercultural communication
- Interest section governance
- Interest section leadership area
- International teaching assistants
- Materials writers
- Program administration
- Refugee concerns
- Research

- Second language writing
- Secondary schools
- Speech, pronunciation, and listening
- Teacher education
- Video and digital media

The activities of several of these sections are discussed more fully in Chapter 3.

Learning the Language

Learning another language is not a prerequisite for most TESOL programs or for most North American or overseas employers. The TESL/TEFL method of instruction is direct English to English. In the United States and Canada, a classroom could have students with a variety of language backgrounds. Having to learn all the different native languages would be unwieldy, to say the least. One ESL teacher in an adult education class in Florida describes her first TESL assignment: "I walked into the classroom and was greeted in a chorus of languages. The majority of the students were from Spanish-speaking countries, but there were several Arabic speakers, one Italian, two or three Farsi speakers, and one Israeli who barely knew the alphabet. They all wanted to converse with me in their native tongue, all hoped that I would learn their language, but it would have been impossible. During the time we had together, we spoke only English. It was amazing watching these people from such diverse cultures using English as a means of communicating with one another."

Although learning another language is not required for obvious reasons, to study at least one strengthens a teacher's employability.

Some professionals feel that ESL/EFL teachers cannot fully understand the problems students encounter studying English unless they have also gone through the process of learning a language themselves. In addition, some employers overseas in countries such as Korea, Japan, or the Arabic-speaking nations give more regard to teachers who have made an effort to learn the language of the host country than to those who never try to do so.

And while English has become the number one international language of business, it is not spoken by every university staff assistant, taxi driver, or store clerk. Knowledge of the language of the country in which you are living and working will make your stay more rewarding.

Volunteering

Many students decide to participate in some kind of volunteer work in an ESL/EFL program just before entering a TESOL training program or while they take the training program as a part of the curriculum. Others who are well-established in the field take time out to help colleagues and cultivate new contacts. "I know from my years of service to TESOL that volunteers can get more out of the experience than they put in," past TESOL president Lydia Stack says. "For example, many of us work in isolation or are professionally undervalued by our employing institutions. However, we TESOL volunteers appreciate one another's skills and ideas. It is a wonderful feeling to realize that you have something to offer other professionals, from surefire classroom techniques, to professional policy suggestions. We can actualize talents and skills we may not even know we have in administration, organization, or communication."

Volunteering is an excellent opportunity to take on new challenges, to prove yourself, and to enhance your effectiveness. It is also an excellent opportunity for making contacts for future employment.

The Cost of Education

While the cost of education continues to escalate, more and more programs are being considered and implemented to help offset the expense. Work-study positions, which could be placements in language centers as practice teachers, are the most prevalent type of assistance. With work-study programs, the burden of the student's salary is shared between the employer and the government, with the student earning the award by working fifteen to twenty hours per week.

Grants and federally insured student loans are also available. Check university financial aid offices for information. (Start at the Department of Education's portal for student aid, http://student aid.ed.gov/PORTALSWebApp/students/english/index.jsp.) A list of links to Canadian provincial financial aid offices can be found at http://canadaonline.about.com/od/studentaid. At the graduate level, teaching assistantships can often provide a stipend and tuition remission and discounts on books and other materials. Check with the individual departments to see what kind of aid they might be able to offer.

TESOL also administers several different programs that offer grants and awards for study or for attending the annual TESOL conference. Contact the TESOL office directly for information.

Many ESL/EFL teachers, after earning their B.A. degrees, work overseas for a number of years, getting a feel for the profession while putting aside funds to finance a master's degree. Although teaching has never been considered a high-paying profession, working abroad in a country with a lower cost of living can help you to earn the money necessary to finance training or to repay student loans more quickly than working in North America would.

Ongoing Professional Development

As good teachers know, training doesn't end once you get your degree or step into your first classroom. It's important to keep up on the latest research and methods in the field through professional organizations, journals, and even an informal teacher network. If you take a job at a large school, you might find yourself with a built-in group of mentors among the other teachers. There are also opportunities for online learning—in both formal courses and through online discussions among teachers. EFL teachers also run a number of blogs, where they chronicle experiences both inside and outside the classroom in a variety of countries. Some employers provide specific training opportunities for teachers.

3

WHAT AN ESL/EFL
TEACHER DOES

ESL/EFL TEACHERS' DUTIES depend, in part, on the institution in which they work, but there are some responsibilities that are common to all settings. ESL/EFL teachers will be responsible for a certain number of classes and will be expected to teach those classes for a certain number of hours per week. In class they must keep track of daily attendance, follow a syllabus, and create and present exercises and activities that facilitate learning. They are also responsible for the atmosphere in the classroom; the teacher's enthusiasm and command of the subject matter should help motivate and inspire confidence in his or her students. Teachers are also expected to manage any discipline problems that occur.

Outside the classroom, teachers are expected to hold office hours for students who have questions or problems. Office hours might also be used to provide students with extra tutoring. Other working hours will be spent designing lesson plans, developing supplemental or primary materials for use in the classroom, writing and grading quizzes and exams, correcting homework assignments, and meeting with coordinators and other teachers in the program. The teacher might also be expected to devote an hour or so a week to supervising language laboratory or library/learning resource center activities.

Work Versus Play

Generally, teachers are contracted to work the academic year— from August or September through May or June. Depending upon the institution, your salary might be for nine months or the full year. This leaves anywhere from sixty to ninety days free for paid or unpaid vacation time. The exception to this is teachers employed by private language centers or businesses that do not follow an academic year. Then vacation time might be as much as thirty or forty-five days, usually paid. Some universities offer students summer sessions, and a teacher can often choose to work for part or all of the summer for extra pay.

Although the work year might be shorter than for most other professions, the daily work load can be as heavy. Primary and secondary school teachers spend their time after classes are through for the day grading papers, designing lesson plans, meeting with parents, supervising after-school activities, and participating in a variety of other duties common to any teaching position.

University teachers might have a less-regular schedule than school teachers, but they still juggle ten to thirty-plus hours a week of classroom teaching with curriculum design, student conferences, materials writing, and committee meetings. Teachers in private language schools often have the heaviest work load, teaching anywhere from twenty-five to forty hours a week. Sometimes they are responsible for a split shift, teaching classes from 8:00 A.M. to noon and then from 4:00 to 8:00 P.M. This can make the day even longer.

Coordinators and supervisors generally teach fewer hours but fill their time with administrative duties, including scheduling, writing course materials and exams, and handling any problems that might arise.

Getting Ahead

ESL/EFL teachers can move up the ladder into administrative positions such as coordinators or program directors. Experienced teachers may choose to advance academically and pursue a Ph.D. degree, getting involved in second language research, presenting papers at seminars and conferences, and writing for professional publications.

They also join the ranks of universities and train future ESL/EFL teachers in master's or certification programs. Teacher-trainers work overseas as well, preparing a country's future teachers to take on the responsibility of ESL/EFL education.

An ESL/EFL professional can take several lateral paths, from research to materials writing and curriculum development.

Administrative Careers

Coordinators/supervisors and program directors are concerned with the overall functioning of a particular program. How many hours a week an administrator will put in is often determined by his or her personality and outlook toward work. Some coordinators and directors spend all their waking hours performing some aspect of their job; others are able to balance the pressures of work with a family or social life. The most organized administrators try to complete as much as they can within a normal forty-hour work week.

Administrators are generally hired on a full-time, salaried basis with an attractive benefits package that could include housing and travel expenses in addition to medical coverage and the usual holidays, vacations, and sick leave. The different types of administrators fall into the following main categories.

Coordinators/Supervisors

Coordinators/supervisors oversee the functioning of a particular segment of the overall program. Within a university language center, for example, they might be responsible for courses offered to arts students or engineering majors.

In addition to possessing the same skills as a classroom teacher, the coordinator or supervisor has other responsibilities:

- Design and develop a course of study appropriate to students' needs and the standards and expectations of the learning institution
- Review and select appropriate ESL/EFL materials
- Coordinate staffing of classes
- Manage group dynamics, which are needed while conducting meetings with students or other teachers and staff members
- Evaluate student abilities and progress through testing and placement tools
- Supervise teachers and professional development

To stay abreast of current teaching methods and to cover sometimes understaffed programs, many coordinators might teach at least one or two classes a week in addition to their other duties.

Program Directors

The title for the top administrative position comes with a variety of designations: program director, director of courses, or director of studies. This administrator is expected to have had a full range of teaching and supervisory experience. In addition to having the required skills for teachers and coordinators, directors are responsible for hiring, providing teacher orientation and training, and observing and evaluating teacher performance. They must manage personnel issues and policies and develop operating procedures. They must adhere to fair practices of recruiting, hiring, and evaluating while encouraging professional development of teachers and staff.

Directors schedule classes, prepare budgets, select and order textbooks, develop student placement and registration procedures, and provide counseling. Directors are also responsible for ensuring ethical practices in recruiting students and disseminating information about the program and its services.

A director must also be able to communicate effectively and have the ability to interact with people of different cultures and personnel at different levels inside and outside the program, including higher authorities, sponsors, students and staff, community and professional organizations and associations and other related interest groups, as well as other colleagues involved with international education.

Directors must see to program structure and decide the number of levels and period lengths, provide student services (settling-in and ongoing orientation programs, Immigration and Naturalization Service regulations), develop and implement missions and goals, adhere to professional standards, and address accreditation issues.

A director might also be involved with marketing, grant writing, data management, and student tracking systems. And, finally, the director might bear responsibility for the physical plant, hiring and supervising maintenance personnel, ordering office equipment and supplies, and dealing with any situations that arise.

Training for Program Administrators

Most program directors come into the field with a background in classroom teaching, as opposed to business and management training. Master's programs in TESOL do not generally provide training for ESL/EFL program administrators. However, several that do include Portland State in Oregon (www.pdx.edu); Georgetown University in Washington, DC (http://college.georgetown.edu); and the University of North Texas in Denton (www.unt.edu). Although the number of administrators is smaller than the number of teachers (and, therefore, openings for these positions are few and far between), it still is important to provide quality training for the person responsible for the overall operation and success of the language program.

Special Interests

Many established TESOLers have chosen a particular interest area to pursue. Some participate in these activities in addition to classroom teaching; others have chosen to leave the classroom to devote more time to these interests. The following are descriptions of the many possible areas of specialty that some ESL/EFL professionals are engaged in.

Research

Researchers address a wide spectrum of problems and questions of interest to ESL/EFL professionals. These topics could range from critical pedagogy (teaching methodology) to analyzing texts and ethnography (a branch of anthropology dealing with the scientific description of individual cultures).

The International Research Foundation for English Language Education (TIRF: www.tirfonline.org), for example, is a group that helps foster new knowledge—and manage existing data—as it relates to teaching and learning English. The foundation offers grants to doctoral candidates and other qualified researchers. In 2005, grant recipients pursed a range of topics, including:

- Listening Too Slowly? The Effect of Rate of Speech in Computer-Delivered Training Sessions for Listening Comprehension in English as a Foreign Language
- Teachers' Beliefs and Practices About the Effective Integration of Grammar Instruction
- An exploratory study of automated essay scoring in an English as a second language (ESL) setting

Other areas that researchers address are issues and concerns in the field of applied linguistics, teacher education, teaching English to deaf students, and curriculum design.

Materials Writers

Although there are thousands of commercially published ESL/EFL textbooks on the market, teachers constantly find themselves having to design materials with the specific needs of their students in mind. Students (and officials) in conservative Arab countries, for example, might take exception to texts depicting the consumption of alcohol or men and women interacting in a way that is not consistent with their own cultural directives. Most published texts don't take these considerations into account.

Often materials are most effective if they are derived from authentic sources and contain cultural themes. To do this commercially would be a daunting enterprise. More often than not, publishers choose books to add to their lists by the size of the market for those books. Material reflecting a specific African culture, for example, while necessary in particular classrooms, might not have a wide enough audience for a publisher to consider taking the project on. In these cases, the ESL/EFL instructor would have to develop his or her own materials.

Another reason to develop your own materials is for use within ESP (English for specific purposes) courses. Appropriate texts might not be available for a group of students studying a particular body of knowledge in English, such as engineering, history, or plant science.

While so many teachers design materials for use in their own classes, there is a broader market for materials writers to expand their talents into writing commercial textbooks. To successfully approach a publisher with a book proposal, a materials writer needs to have a little market savvy. Being aware of books that have already been published can help you to identify the gaps in the marketplace. Once you have identified a gap, your proposal should be designed to convince a publisher that your book idea would fill that gap.

Areas where people have successfully published books include the following:

- Teacher training materials
- Guides for teaching vocabulary, writing, computer research, grammar, and so on
- Critical theory and pedagogy
- ESL activity books
- Family and workplace situation literacy materials

You have heard the expression, "No need to reinvent the wheel," but so many eager materials writers forget that basic principle. Often time and energy are expended creating materials for a particular course of study or for a proposal to a publisher when a flood of perfectly good textbooks on the subject already exists. Study existing textbooks and note who the publishers are. For help in designing your book proposal, refer to Michael Larsen's book *How to Write a Book Proposal* (Writer's Digest Books, 2004).

English for Specific Purposes

The term ESP (English for specific purposes) encompasses a number of areas. One such area is EAP (English for academic purposes), which refers to any course of study in an academic environment, from psychology to theology or history.

ESP also has uses outside an educational setting—focusing on usage in the business community or legal arena, for example. There are interesting debates within the profession whether a content background is necessary to teach ESP. For example, does an instructor teaching English for medical purposes need to have a medical background?

Some teachers feel they must have a working knowledge of each discipline to teach it in English. In some cases, this concern is valid;

a teacher providing support to the medical program, for example, would have to be familiar with certain terminology to teach it. In some university settings, ESP instructors are required to sit in and take notes in the classes they are supporting. This can add to schedule loads, but it also helps alleviate anxiety. It is important to remember that in whatever context you are teaching, you are ultimately responsible for English-language concepts.

Another debate is whether classes should be separated by discipline as opposed to grouping a variety of topics together. Can you effectively teach content-based ESP courses to engineering and medical students in the same classroom?

Test Preparation

One area of ESP is providing prep courses for students needing to take English-language proficiency tests. These tests are used by administrators to help with decisions regarding admission to universities, level placement in language programs, eligibility for educational grants and awards, or certain licenses. Some ESL/EFL instructors work only with test preparation, teaching the particular skills necessary to do well on the following exams:

Test of English as a Foreign Language (TOEFL)

TOEFL is used mainly to assess language proficiency in North American English and placement levels for incoming international students to U.S. universities and colleges. In addition, government and certification agencies use the scores to determine a person's proficiency in English. It measures listening comprehension, structure and written expression, and vocabulary and reading comprehension. In 2005 a number of countries, including the United States and Canada, began to use an Internet-based TOEFL test to better capture speech patterns and standardize responses. The test is administered in 180 countries around the world at testing centers, colleges, and universities.

Test of Written English (TWE)

TWE assesses the English writing proficiency of non-native English speakers. It is an essay test that is administered six times a year as part of the TOEFL exam. Its scores are used by undergraduate and graduate programs for admissions purposes. TWE measures writing skills that focus on sentence structure, syntax, ability to present ideas in an organized fashion, and ability to choose appropriate details to support a thesis. Here is a sample essay question taken from a previous TWE: "Inventions such as eyeglasses and the sewing machine have had an important effect on our lives. Choose another invention that you think is important. Give specific reasons for your choice."

Test of English for International Communication (TOEIC)

TOEIC measures listening and reading comprehension and the proficiency of non-native speakers engaged in business, commerce, and industry. Open testing is held twelve times a year at different locations.

Test of Spoken English (TSE)

TSE assesses spoken English proficiency. It is an oral free-response test offered twelve times a year around the world. It is used mainly to determine eligibility for graduate teaching assistantships and professional licensing. TSE measures the candidates' skills in reading aloud, proper pronunciation and clear speech, telling a story, and answering questions.

Secondary Level English Proficiency Test (SLEP)

SLEP assesses the English listening and reading comprehension proficiency of secondary school students who are non-native speakers of English. It is used to determine progress and readiness to enter into full-time instructional programs conducted in English. This multiple-choice test is administered locally.

Institutional Testing Program (TOEFL ITP)

ITP offers an unofficial TOEFL-format exam (composed of previously administered paper-based TOEFL tests) for those pursuing academic studies. Available on demand, the ITP is administered by individual institutions, and results are used for placement and admissions purposes.

Test-preparation instructors work in university-based language centers, in private language schools, in adult education programs, and in community colleges.

4

SALARIES AND BENEFITS

To TEACHERS OF any subject or level, be it kindergarten or graduate school, one of the main sources of satisfaction is working with students, guiding their progress through a set of goals, measuring their achievement with exams or papers or other devices, then sending them on their way with the hope that the knowledge imparted will prove useful.

With some subjects, though, such as history or calculus, teachers never learn whether the information they have provided and the skills they have taught will, indeed, have an impact on the student's future. However, teachers of English to nonnative speakers have the added benefit of knowing that their students are studying English because their need for it is immediate. Whether to continue their studies or function in business or in day-to-day life in a new country, mastering English to at least some degree of competency becomes crucial to their success. The ESL/EFL teacher plays a large part in helping to bring that about.

See the World

There are other rewards of the TESOL profession that, to some teachers, are even more valuable than working with students. Travel tops the list for many. But it is not just the opportunity to travel that makes the profession so attractive; it is the chance to live for long periods of time in a variety of foreign countries.

Even teachers who choose to stay in the United States or Canada but who are prepared to move to another city and state can benefit from the diverse cultures they come in contact with in their home country. Here are some comments on the subject of travel from a few different longtime ESL/EFL teachers.

> "I enjoy living as a guest in another country where I can see the world from a completely different perspective."
> "The way of doing things is novel, and it's a challenge because it's not what you're used to."
> "It forces you to look at yourself in a different way."
> "I like the opportunity to get to know people from other cultures and to get to know them fairly closely, more so than when you're just a tourist."
> "As well as imparting something they consider of value— the English language—you can get a lot back, learning about the different ways people look at things."
> "[Teaching EFL] . . . has allowed me to see and do things I never would have been able to do otherwise."
> "[Travel] . . . gets in your blood; I have a real fascination for other cultures and languages."
> "I like the flexibility of being able to change jobs and locations every so often."

"You can live overseas in a country for a number of years
and really get to know what it's like in depth."

Along with getting to know the host country well, ESL/EFL
teachers also get the opportunity to visit other parts of the world.
Some employers provide an air ticket at the beginning and at the
end of a contract, and some even provide a yearly ticket to travel
home during the long summer vacation or to trade in for tickets to
countries closer to the work location. Many overseas travel agents
can help teachers find bargain package deals. For example, from
Muscat, Oman, a plane trip to Bangkok costs as little as $400, with
accommodation in a four-star hotel available for less than $100 a
night. Imagine what a trip would cost from any point within the
United States or Canada.

Around-the-world tickets, which are often available for a few
thousand dollars, can be a good way to stretch your travel budget.
These are also less expensive when purchased in, say, Bangkok
rather than North America. After a few years overseas, the dollars
start mounting up in the savings account, and so does the frequent
flyer mileage. ESL/EFL teachers not only have the time to travel,
they often have the means as well.

U.S. Salaries

Teaching, in general, has never been considered one of the highest-
paying professions, and that holds true for TESOL. Certified ESL
teachers working within a public school system in the United States
are paid following the same scale of teachers of other subjects.
Although pay scales vary widely depending upon the region of the

country in which a teacher works, the average starting salary for a beginning teacher is about $31,000 annually. ESL teachers in private schools can earn even less.

According to a report released by the National Education Association, the average salary of all teachers (2004–2005) was $47,750 a year.

ESL teachers working in private language schools or university language centers for incoming international students can be hired on a full-time basis and paid a yearly salary or hired part-time and paid an hourly wage for each period of instruction. Adult education and community college instructors teaching ESL generally are part-time and are usually paid by the course.

Some positions, especially those affiliated with universities, offer a yearly salary paid out over a nine-month period—the academic year. Depending on the dollar amount, such an arrangement could leave you scrambling for a supplemental income during the school year or force you to give up your long July and August vacation to teach summer school. Be sure to have your calculator handy when the salary offer is made.

Canadian Salaries

In Canada, public schools are operated by individual provinces and territories, so policies and salaries can vary widely in different parts of the country. ESL teachers, however, can get a general salary range from the Canadian Teachers' Federation (www.ctf-fce.ca). According to CTF, Canadian teacher salaries are typically based on postsecondary education, experience, and any additional administrative duties.

An entry-level teacher with a college education can expect to earn anywhere from $34,000 to $52,000 a year. As a teacher moves up the experience ladder, that range maxes out anywhere from $50,000 to $72,000 a year. Teachers who don't hold degrees can expect lower salaries than the ones listed above, while those with graduate degrees or other specialized training can earn higher ones.

Unfortunately, adult ESL positions tend to be part-time or seasonal and are generally hourly. According to an occupational profile from the Alberta Learning Information Service, hourly rates for adult ESL teachers range from $15 to $40 in the private sector and $30 to $50 for positions at public institutions.

Money Abroad

Salaries and benefits vary from region to region and employer to employer. In general, jobs in areas that present more "hardship" for Americans or Canadians, such as Persian Gulf countries or countries with thriving economies, pay higher wages and provide more allowances. In poorer countries salaries tend to be lower.

No matter which country you work in, if you meet certain requirements, such as the length of time spent out of the United States or Canada, you will not be required to pay U.S. or Canadian income tax. This can substantially increase the face value of your overseas salary. But be sure to inquire whether the country where you have been offered a job levies an income tax against its residents and foreign workers. This can make a big difference in calculating the overall salary package.

Teacher salaries vary widely depending on the country and an individual teacher's experience. Even within a single country, pay can vary widely among different schools, as well as urban versus rural settings. Browsing online job ads, some of which include salary ranges, can help you get a handle on a specific country. Another good idea is to get in touch with teachers already working in a particular country. Many websites provide forums where teachers exchange tips and information. See Appendix A for some popular sites to get started. Some of the highest-paid jobs are in the Middle East and Asia in such countries as Japan, Saudi Arabia, and Taiwan.

For those working overseas, there is one other consideration to take into account regarding finances. If you are being paid in a currency other than U.S. or Canadian dollars (which is very likely), you should make sure the country in which you are planning to work has a free currency exchange. In some parts of the world where dollars are hard to come by, governments prohibit currency exchange or limit the amount that can be changed into dollars. A salary that is not convertible to dollars will not allow you to save any money for use in the rest of the world.

For current exchange rates, check the newspaper or consult with your bank. There are also a variety of currency calculators online. You choose one country's currency (say the United States or Canada) and a second country for an up-to-date exchange rate. A good place to start is www.bankrate.com. Simply type "currency converter" into the site's search box to bring up the currency calculator. Keep in mind that when you actually change money, there will be a fee involved in addition to the exchange rate. These fees vary quite a bit depending on where you change money. Shop around for the best rates.

If your salary is 100 percent transferable, as it should be, make sure that you arrange for regular wire transfers/deposits to your account at your home bank. The country in which you are working might not have government-insured banking, and you don't want to risk losing your hard-earned dollars. Many teachers caught during the 1990 Iraqi invasion of Kuwait can testify to that.

Benefits in the United States

As already mentioned, your benefits package will largely be determined by whether you are paid on a full-time basis or with a part-time hourly wage. Full-time ESL teachers working within a school system receive the same benefits as other teachers. This can include medical coverage, paid vacation and sick days, some sort of continuing education allowance, banking privileges with a credit union, and a retirement plan.

Full-time ESL teachers at universities or language schools can expect similar benefits. It is the part-time instructor who generally does not benefit from any additional perks. This needs to be considered when analyzing job offers (See Chapter 5).

Benefits in Canada

Full-time ESL teachers working within a province or territory school system receive the same benefits as other teachers. Fringe benefits might include compassionate leave, supplementary medical insurance, cumulative sick leave, long-term disability insurance, maternity leave, retirement gratuities, sabbatical and study leave, life insurance, and dental insurance.

Teachers generally contribute anywhere from 7 to 10 percent of their salaries to a required retirement program. Pensions are then awarded to retired teachers based on years of service and average salary. In addition, many of these retirement plans include benefits for disabled teachers or the surviving family members of deceased teachers.

Benefits Overseas

Experienced TESOLers are well aware of the standard benefit packages many overseas employers offer and know that they can substantially increase an otherwise unglamorous salary. As mentioned earlier in this chapter, some employers provide a plane ticket to and from your home city at the beginning and end of your contract. Others might offer a flight bonus at the end of your contract or pay for your return flight after a specified number of months. These benefits vary widely by employer.

Here are some other standard benefits you can expect from an overseas employer.

Housing

In some parts of the world, such as Asia or the Middle East, rentals run extremely high, so often the employer provides free housing. Some universities or private companies maintain their own complexes of staff housing, apartment buildings, or small houses or villas; if they don't, they might subsidize employees with a housing allowance. This can be a plus, giving teachers a choice of location and type of housing away from the compound-style living many find too limiting. The allowance usually is enough to cover the rental costs; if you shop around, there might even be something left over. But be sure to investigate current rental rates in advance. (You can contact a previous or current employee or check with the country's embassy.) And, often, landlords expect several months' rent up front. Find out if your employer is prepared to cover this cost for you.

Furnishings

Again, what is provided in the way of furnishings varies from job to job. Most employers supply at least the basic pieces—beds, tables, lamps. If not, ask if they provide a furniture allowance. Before you go, check to see if kitchen items and bedding and towels are part of the deal. If they are not, it is usually easier and less expensive to buy what you need there rather than have everything shipped from home. Sometimes teachers leaving the country sell secondhand basics at a good price.

Utilities

Some jobs include the cost of utilities as part of the housing benefit. Others might offer an electricity allowance. Generally, teachers are responsible for their own telephone bills.

Baggage Allowance

Many employers offer some sort of baggage allowance for the cost of shipping personal items. This is usually paid after you have arrived. Someone just starting out might wisely choose to travel light, but after the first year or so overseas, many teachers find their need for a baggage allowance has increased with their possessions. Some employers provide a settling-in allowance in lieu of or in addition to a baggage allowance. This can run from one-half month's salary on up.

Transportation

Very few employers of ESL/EFL teachers provide cars or car allowances, although they will often provide transportation to and from the work site. Many teachers, depending upon where they are living and working, purchase their own cars or rely on public transportation to get around.

Medical Coverage

Some countries offer their residents as well as foreign workers free government-sponsored medical care as part of their social structure. In other countries a teacher might be on his or her own. It is a good idea to check into insurance policies that can cover you while traveling out of the country. U.S.-based TESOL members can qualify for health insurance while living in the United States or working abroad. Canadians should look into purchasing a private insurance policy to cover them while living in a foreign country. While Canada has government-provided health care, those benefits are limited when citizens travel or live outside the country.

Allowances for Dependents

If you are married and want your family to relocate with you, make sure that your job is offering you a "married status" position. Some employers will take on teachers only in a "single status" capacity and either won't provide housing or tickets for dependents or won't allow them to accompany you, even if you are able to pay for them.

If the position is for "married status," you might receive beginning and end-of-contract tickets and leave tickets for your spouse and possibly up to three children.

If you do plan to have your children with you, remember to check whether the employer offers an education allowance. The tuition for international schools overseas can run quite high.

End-of-Contract Gratuity

Some countries (again, particularly in the Persian Gulf) offer a bonus at the end of the employment contract. This can amount to half a month's salary for each year of service.

Benefits Not Offered

Foreign employers rarely offer retirement plans or permanent job security. They also will not make payments into your Social Security account. If you stay overseas for a long period, you will not qualify for these benefits when you retire unless you have contributed to the fund during a certain number of quarters in your working career. Check with the Social Security Administration (www.ssa.gov) for specifics.

What Does It All Add Up To?

Working overseas can provide a substantial monetary increase over salaries in the United States or Canada, but only if you look at the numbers closely. Take a typical entry-level teacher salary ($31,000 in the United States, or roughly $40,000 in Canada), and add up what you now pay in rent and utilities each year. Those expenses disappear for many overseas teachers, who receive housing as a job benefit. It's a perk that can increase the value of your overall salary package by thousands of dollars a year.

It's also helpful to add in the value of the extras often provided to English teachers overseas. There's often a round-trip plane ticket, which can be worth $1,200 or more, as well as a year-end bonus. The latter is often worth a month's salary and can add another $2,500 or so to the overall package. These are projected estimates, but you can see that a salary overseas, even one significantly lower than $31,000, might actually be worth a great deal more than if you worked in North America.

Teacher salaries will generally increase the longer you stay overseas, and it's important to factor in the local cost of living. The English-speaking section of Foreign Language Teachers United offers a table to help you figure out what might be a fair wage in a variety of countries (www.efltu.org/articles.htm). In addition to all the other rewards of the TESOL profession, the financial benefits can be very attractive.

5

JOB HUNTING

TEACHER SUPPLY AND demand, as in other professions, is affected by economic and social conditions. Each decade sees a different trend, from the need for teachers in general to the need for those in specific subject areas. To stay informed of current trends, good sources of information are the reports that the research divisions of the National Education Association (NEA), the Department of Labor, and the U.S. Department of Education release. The Organization for Economic Co-operation and Development (OECD) charts the needs of schools and subject areas on an international scale. These statistics are available at libraries or by contacting the individual organizations. (See Appendix A.)

Do Your Homework

Seasoned TESOLers follow a series of well-proven methods that take the guesswork out of job hunting. Once a newcomer learns the ropes, finding that second or third job becomes a much simpler process.

Steps to locate employment can begin not at the end of your studies but while you are choosing the training program you will attend. Most universities with TESOL programs have an on-site language center or offer ESL classes to incoming international students where you can volunteer your services or be placed for practice teaching. In addition, many U.S. universities operate EFL programs with sister universities in foreign countries, such as Malaysia or Indonesia. After graduation you might be able to slip into a full-time job through your own program.

Once you are enrolled in your TESOL program, try to absorb as much information as you possibly can. Take advantage of your college or university's graduate placement office. Counselors maintain books and pamphlets on specific careers and can help guide you to the appropriate resources. And remember to discuss your plans with your professors. Most will be actively involved in the field, keeping in touch with other professionals. The contacts you make during your training program can be invaluable for future job placement.

Joining Professional Associations

TESOL (Teachers of English to Speakers of Other Languages) is the predominant professional association for ESL/EFL teachers. Membership, in addition to keeping you abreast of current developments in the field, will help you in your job search. The organization features an online job bank for employers and prospective employees, listing openings both in the United States and overseas, as well as a number of publications offering an overview of the field.

Originally called the National Association of Foreign Student Advisers and now renamed the Association of International Educators, NAFSA is an organization encouraging international education and providing professional development opportunities for those in the field. It has a strong ESL/EFL connection, and its weekly e-mail newsletter (*NAFSA.news*) provides updates on federal policy, professional conferences, and other developments in international education.

Help Wanted

Although standard help-wanted ads found in local newspapers might be of some help locating employment close to home, most TESOL professionals are prepared to relocate. The opportunity to travel, whether within the United States or overseas, is still one of the most attractive benefits of the profession.

With that in mind, there are specific periodicals TESOLers regularly use in their employment search. In addition to the job bulletins published by TESOL and NAFSA, there are several other good sources of ESL/EFL job listings. The website for *The Chronicle of Higher Education*, a professional journal published weekly, features the Chronicle Careers job bank, which advertises openings both in the United States and abroad. UK newspapers (as well as their online job banks) are worth investigating as well because many overseas employers look to England to find teachers. A good place to start is the *Times Educational Supplement* (www.tes.co.uk).

Here are some sample advertisements for job openings found through the previously mentioned sources. Because these particular positions are no longer vacant, the hiring institutions are not identified.

Iowa

English as a Second Language, one (1) 2-year term renewable instructorship.

Duties: Teach ESL for academic purposes; assist in ESL curriculum development/research. Required: MA in TESOL or the equivalent; 2 years' teaching experience overseas or in intensive English program. Salary: commensurate with education and experience plus benefits for academic year. $27,200 minimum. Summer employment is possible. Send letter of interest, CV, 3 letters of reference.

California

Position: ESL High School Teacher. Duties: Classroom instruction. Requirements: Valid California secondary credential authorizing ESL or bilingual instruction. Qualifications: Appropriate student teaching or equivalent. Salary: Dependent upon experience and references. Benefits: Health, dental, and vision insurance. Starts: August.

China

Public school. Position: Primary and secondary ESL teacher. Jilin Province in northern China needs English-language educators to share and impart their skills to eager students. Positions on offer are to teach English to students aged between 5 and 16 who are learning English full-time in their branches in government schools throughout Jilin. The commitment expected from you is 5 to 6 days a week, no more than 85 teaching hours per month. Curriculum and teaching material will be provided.

Depending on your qualification, you could be earning between 4,000 to 5,000 Yuan Renminbi ($500 to $625) per month with overtime compensation. Work visa will be sponsored before you depart for China and accident and health coverage will be offered to you. Modern Western accommodation facilities will be supplied. Airfare to the amount of 7,000 Yuan Renminbi will be reimbursed immediately upon completion of your one-year contract. You DO NOT need to have a tertiary qualified degree or a TESOL certificate to secure these positions. We want Native English Speakers who have enthusiasm in teaching English to Chinese learners. If you are adventurous and would like more information, please contact . . .

Documents needed upon applying:

- Résumé
- A recent photograph of you
- Photocopy of your passport
- Photocopy of your degree/s or diploma/s if you have
- Photocopy of a recent medical check-up report

Germany

Private language institute. Position: Teacher/trainer. We have been one of the leading language schools in Düsseldorf for more than fifteen years and are looking for TESL/TEFL–certified native English speakers to handle about 30 hours a week of classes. We offer international language courses as well as language study tours abroad to Europe, USA, Australia, and Cuba. Students include both individuals and businesspeople. You must possess knowledge of and interest in e-learning, flexibility, and excellent communications skills, and an ability to update Newsboards. We can offer a one-year contract and guarantee a minimum salary of 1,200 Euro (about $1,500) per month.

Job Hunting Online

If you have online access, you can take advantage of other electronic job banks when searching for a position. (See Appendix A for a list of sites to get you started.)

NAFSA's website is also a source for ESL/EFL job openings. Its job registry features job postings in the areas of overseas opportunities, international student services, and much more. Members can post résumés on the site, and employers can search for potential candidates.

TESL-L is an electronic discussion forum for practitioners of TESL/TEFL. Free to anyone who subscribes, it also includes several specialized discussion groups, including TESP-L (English for Special Purposes) and TESLJB-L (information on jobs and employment issues). To participate in TESL-L and any of its branches, send a message to listserv@cunyvm.cuny.edu. In the body of the message, write SUB TESL-L your first name, your last name (SUB TESL-L Joe Smith), or check the website for more information (www.hunter.cuny.edu/~tesl-l).

Going to Conferences

TESOL holds an annual convention and exhibit that is well attended (more than nine thousand TESOLers travel from afar to this yearly event) by teachers, program developers, and administrators, many of whom are also there to find employment—or employees. In fact, the annual TESOL convention is one of the best ways to secure an ESL/EFL job.

In addition to the various speakers, presentations, and other professional development opportunities the TESOL conference offers, there are also pre- and postconvention institutes and job workshops providing career development advice. Space is set aside each year where hiring institutions can post their job openings and study résumés of prospective candidates. Private spaces are made available for face-to-face interviews, which can result in on-the-spot job offers. A large number of seasoned ESL/EFL teachers can claim at least one position secured by this means.

TESOL affiliates (autonomous organizations with a separate membership from TESOL) also hold regional conferences throughout the United States at different times in the year. Recruiters attend these events as well, although on a smaller scale than the annual convention. TESOL's central office can locate an affiliate contact near you.

NAFSA's annual convention also attracts job recruiters.

International Schools Services (ISS) is a nonprofit corporation dedicated to excellence for children attending overseas schools worldwide (see the discussion on ISS in the following section). However, it should be noted that ISS sponsors four International Recruitment Centers (IRCs)—three-day recruitment conferences—annually. They're held in the United States and overseas. During this time, overseas administrators make recruitment trips to fill their staffing needs. On average, each IRC hosts thirty-five to forty international schools seeking to fill teaching and administrative positions. About 50 percent of job seekers who attend ultimately accept a position from the conference. Active ISS candidates may register and schedule interviews with prospective employers. ISS placed more than seven hundred teachers and administrators in 2005. It reports that 82 percent of its placements secure their positions at one of the IRCs.

Employment Agencies

There are many legitimate private employment agencies that deal exclusively with teaching and related positions. As a job seeker, you will usually be asked to fill out an application and provide several copies of your résumé, diplomas/credentials, letters of reference, and state-preferred geographical locations. You will also be asked to pay a registration/service fee. When signing up with an agency, it is best to go with an organization whose reputation you are familiar with. There are many fly-by-night employment agencies to watch out for. Here are some of the warning signs:

- They charge exorbitant fees.
- They inform you of just the right job opening and ask you to pay a deposit "in good faith" to hold the job for you.
- They make unsubstantiated claims, such as promising a woman a no-strings-attached EFL position in Saudi Arabia. (Women may teach in Saudi Arabia but have to abide by certain restrictions.)

You will find a list of selected employment contacts in Appendixes A and B.

As mentioned earlier, International Schools Services (ISS) is a nonprofit corporation. Founded in 1955, ISS is committed to fostering excellence in education for children attending schools overseas. ISS headquarters is in Princeton, New Jersey, and is staffed by professional personnel experienced in international education. ISS provides services to overseas schools including recruitment and recommendation of personnel, curricular and administrative guidance, school management, materials procurement, financial management, consulting services, and publications. Services to job candidates, in addition to the IRCs, include a year-round placement program for vacancies that occur in the late spring, summer, and midyear.

The American and international schools using the ISS recruitment service are attended by a multinational student body of the children of international business and diplomatic personnel. Schools are located throughout Africa, Asia, Central and South America, Europe, and the Middle East. The language of instruction is English, and the curriculum follows a standard U.S. program. Because many of the children come from families where English is not the native language, opportunities exist for ESL teachers.

ISS will accept candidates with a bachelor's degree or higher and at least two years of current, successful, full-time elementary or secondary school experience. (The two years' experience is sometimes waived for certain situations.) Although ISS does not require teaching certification, many of the schools that recruit through ISS do.

Because the number of applicants for administrative positions exceeds the number of available jobs, administrators with previous overseas work experience are in a better position to be offered jobs.

ISS applicants pay a modest registration fee, which covers processing of the registration packet and review of the applicant's qualifications. ISS does not charge a placement fee.

For more information and an application write to:

International Schools Services
15 Roszel Road, P.O. Box 5910
Princeton, New Jersey 08543
www.iss.edu

The Direct Approach

Institutions, particularly smaller ones overseas, do not always advertise their openings in the United States or Canada through the usual channels. If there is a particular country in which you hope to work or a particular institution to which you would like to apply, it can be advantageous to make a direct approach.

Your library can help you with listings of domestic and overseas schools, universities, and language centers. For overseas institutions, you can also write or telephone a specific country's embassy in Washington, DC, and ask for its educational/cultural affairs office. Often the officer in charge of that department also plays some role in the recruitment procedure and will know of any openings in his or her home country.

Networking

Word-of-mouth is still one of the most effective ways to learn of job openings, particularly in the TESOL profession. You can find other ESL/EFL teachers in your own program or at regional and national conventions. Talk to these other teachers and find out where they have worked and how to go about applying. Former or current employees of a particular institution can be a wealth of information about employment and living conditions.

Traveling "On Spec"

Some more intrepid TESOLers have traveled to their location of choice with the hope of finding employment upon arrival. In some countries, such as Thailand, this can be a successful method, securing teaching on a part-time basis in local language schools or finding individual students to tutor privately. However, it is a risky proposition. More and more language schools seek professional candidates through the normal channels, and if your travel and living expenses depend upon finding employment, you could find yourself a long way from home without funds.

There are also a few other disadvantages to this method. Many employers expecting to hire staff from the United States or United

Kingdom also expect to pay for air tickets, accommodations, and other expenses such as baggage and settling-in allowances. By arriving unannounced on an employer's doorstep, you might be short-changing yourself an attractive salary and benefits package. In addition, work visas in some countries can be obtained only when the candidate is outside the country. You could arrive, find a job, then discover that you have to leave again to satisfy work and immigration regulations. And, finally, some countries, such as those in the Middle East, will deny you entry unless you have a work visa or a sponsor (an employer) in advance (see Chapter 9).

How to Apply

Once you have learned where the jobs are and what the conditions and salary will be, there are certain steps to follow when submitting your application.

Important Documents

In addition to your résumé and cover letter, there are certain documents you will need to have when sending out applications. You will need a good supply of photocopies of your diplomas, certificates, or teaching credentials. You will need copies of letters of reference (most employers want to see at least three), certified copies of transcripts, and a good supply of passport-size photos, available through a photography studio or from a coin-operated booth.

Some overseas employers might also want to see birth certificates, marriage licenses, and documents for all dependents. In addition, for overseas applications, you will have to provide a photocopy of a current passport. For more information on passports, visas, and other documents, see Chapter 7.

Writing the Cover Letter

A cover letter is often your first introduction to a potential employer, and it must make a good impression. Cover letters should be typed on good bond paper and be neat and free of mistakes. They should be addressed to a specific person by name and should be tailor-made for each job. In as few words as possible, mention your most relevant experience or qualifications up front and that you are offering your services for employment. Don't neglect to mention the job for which you are applying; an institution could be advertising more than one position. Finally, don't mention the résumé you have enclosed until you are ready to sign off. If you refer to it too soon, the reader will probably turn to it before finishing your letter.

Designing Your Résumé

Your résumé should reflect your qualifications and your experience in the best possible light. As with your cover letter, your résumé should be on good paper and be error-free. If your qualifications outweigh your experience, present that section first. If you have been in the field for a while and have some impressive experience you want to showcase, then the education/qualifications section can be placed second. List your experience beginning with your most recent position, and try to keep your résumé to no more than two pages.

Many experienced job hunters use a "skills summary" section to highlight their area of special expertise. See the sample résumé in Figure 5.1 for overseas job hunting.

Figure 5.1 Sample Résumé for Overseas Job Hunting

Name (first, middle, last)

Address

Telephone (country code–1–and area code)

E-mail address

Skills Summary

Teaching: ESL/EFL-conversation, reading, comprehension, grammar, listening, writing

Specializations: English for Special Purposes—medicine, engineering; CALL, computer-assisted language learning

Writing: ESL/EFL and ESP materials

Languages: Fluency in French, knowledge of Spanish

Administrative: Course coordination, program development, scheduling

Technical: Any special computer skills, such as HTML proficiency

Education

University name, city and state, year graduated, master's degree

University name, city and state, year graduated, bachelor's degree

Experience

Institution name, city and state, country

Job title, starting date/ending date

Duties

Institution name, city and state, country

Job title, starting date/ending date

Duties

Affiliations

TESOL, NAFSA

If you have an extensive background, you may decide to list your qualifications in a curriculum vitae, or CV (from the Latin meaning "course of life"). A CV is generally longer than a résumé and covers your experience and accomplishments in more depth, including the following sections.

Key Qualifications

Summarize your experience and training most relevant to the position sought. Describe degree of responsibility held on previous assignments, giving dates and locations (up to half a page).

Education

Use up to a quarter page and list university degrees and any specialized training programs, giving names of institutions, degrees or certificates obtained, and dates attended.

Experience Record

Use up to three-quarters of a page and list all positions held since graduation with job titles, locations, duties performed, and dates. Give names of references where appropriate.

Other Skills

Mention language proficiency and any other job-related skills.

Related Activities

Summarize any related activities such as volunteer and committee work.

Summary of Publications

Provide a brief list of any relevant publications, technical articles, or reports.

Awards/Honors

List any academic, job-related, or community awards. This is also a good place to list any grants or fellowships.

Résumé Dos and Don'ts

The information you include (or don't include) on your résumé depends a great deal upon whether the job for which you are applying is at home or abroad. In North America, equal-opportunity laws protect job seekers from being discriminated against on the basis of age, sex, race, religion, ethnic background, and marital status. This information—your birth date; whether you are divorced, married, or single; how many dependents you have; your nationality—is never included on a résumé intended for a domestic job search.

However, if you are applying for jobs overseas, it is important to include this information. Antidiscrimination laws do not always exist in other countries, and employers sometimes base their hiring decisions on these vital statistics. It is not necessarily so that they may better discriminate against you. Some employers provide air tickets and other allowances for accompanying spouses and dependents.

You should also remember to include your gender on résumés going overseas. Your name isn't necessarily a clue to an overseas employer, and often certain positions at certain institutions, especially in the Middle East, are quite specific as to the sex of a candidate they are seeking—and are able to hire. (More on that subject in Chapter 9.)

Finally, it is not necessary to include your religion on your résumé, but you might later be asked to divulge that information on visa applications or airport landing cards or on some other official documents.

Interview Savvy

Your cover letter and résumé help an employer get to know you, at least on paper, but the personal interview is what can clinch the deal. This is your chance to show your intelligence, your poise and confidence, your manner and style of speaking—in essence, your personality. Of course, being well groomed is a given, no matter whether the job you are applying for is a Fortune 500 company or a tiny village school in the jungle of Central Africa.

Here are a few tips to help the interview go smoothly:

- Come prepared with a mental list of questions, but don't ask them until invited to do so.
- Your questions should focus on the job itself, duties, and responsibilities rather than the salary and perks. Let the interviewer bring up the subject of benefits. (Then ask your questions.)
- Demonstrate interest by making eye contact with the interviewer; don't let your attention roam around the room.

Many newcomers to the TESOL field are surprised to learn that a good number of overseas job offers come with the candidate's never being invited for an interview. The distances and expense involved often make personal interviews impossible. An employer might conduct an interview over the telephone or offer you a job through the mail on the weight of your documents alone.

Following Up

A thank-you note is a thoughtful and practical gesture after an interview. It lets the interviewer know that your interest is still keen and serves as a memory jogger. And even if you have decided that the position is not one you wish to pursue, it is still a good idea to follow up with a written thank-you. Down the road, the contacts you have developed can pay off.

Evaluating the Job Offer

You have completed your TESOL program, attended conferences, made your contacts, studied the job advertisements, and sent out your applications, and now the job offers are starting to come in. But how do you know which job will be right for you? There are several elements you need to examine and weigh, balancing the salary and benefits with the cost of living, the actual work you will be doing, under what conditions, and what your living arrangements and lifestyle will be.

You also need to consider the length of the contract being offered and whether it is renewable, how much you will need to spend to get settled in—for example, if a car is necessary, if the accommodations are fully or only partially furnished—and how many tickets home per year are provided. (See Chapter 7 for important questions to ask before you accept a job offer overseas and the steps involved in the hiring process.)

Table 5.1 indicates the areas of importance for one particular applicant who interviewed for three positions at the annual TESOL convention.

While it appears that the salary in Japan is the highest, the applicant's research revealed that the cost of living was also the highest. Because it was important for her to be able to travel home easily to the United States at least once a year, without a vacation ticket as part of the benefit package, she eliminated the Japan job offer.

Table 5.1 An Applicant's Job Factors for Three TESOL Positions

	Job A	Job B	Job C
Location	Japan	South Korea	Oman
Setting	Private Company	University	University
Materials	Provided	Not Provided	Provided
Student Level	Adult Engineers	Freshmen	Freshmen
Annual Salary	$40,000	$31,000	$33,000
Accommodations	Yes	Yes (Shared)	Yes
Cost of Living	Very High	Moderate	High
Air Tickets	Provided	Provided	Provided
Vacation Tickets	Not Provided	Provided	Provided
Benefits Package	Yes	Yes	Yes
Teaching Hours	25 Contact	25 Contact	18 to 20 Contact
	10 Office	10 Office	18 to 20 Office/
	(Split Shift)		Research
Additional Responsibilities	None	Research Materials/ Curriculum Design	Research Materials/ Curriculum Design

The job offers from South Korea and Oman appeared equal in almost every way. At the convention she was able to track down teachers currently working in both settings, all of whom gave favorable reports. In the end, she chose South Korea because of its proximity to countries she had been hoping to visit.

Knowing your priorities and gathering appropriate information will help you to make informed decisions. But whatever the decision you ultimately make, at some point you will realize that you are not just evaluating and finally taking a job offer. You have been presented with a valuable gift. A job in TESOL opens up the entire world to you, contributing to your financial security and leading you to personal and professional growth.

6

U.S. and Canadian Teaching Jobs

There's an extremely positive employment climate for ESL teachers in the United States. According to the National Clearinghouse for English Language Acquisition & Language Instruction Educational Programs (NCELA), the number of English-language learners enrolled in K–12 in the United States increased more than 65 percent between the 1993–94 school year and the 2003–4 school year.

According to the U.S. Department of Labor, Bureau of Labor Statistics, there's a growing demand for qualified teachers to make sure these students become proficient in English. The bureau reports:

> Currently, many school districts have difficulty hiring qualified teachers in some subject areas—most often mathematics, science (especially chemistry and physics), bilingual education, and foreign languages. Increasing enrollments of minorities, coupled with a shortage of minority teachers, should cause efforts to recruit

minority teachers to intensify. Also, the number of non-English-speaking students will continue to grow, creating demand for bilingual teachers and for those who teach English as a second language.

In Canada, the job outlook is mixed. The general employment projections for secondary and university teachers are generally listed from good to fair by various government entities and studies. Modest job growth is expected in these sectors, which will be supplemented by openings left by large numbers of retirees over the next decade. In addition, Canada's urban school boards have seen an influx of immigrants with a need for quality ESL education. Some school boards, however, haven't been as fast to react to these changes as ESL professionals would like. A research paper published by TESL Ontario, for example, is titled *Myths and Delusions: The State of ESL in Large Canadian School Boards*. It describes how Canadian schools have failed to provide qualified ESL teachers for all the students who need them.

Working Conditions

Workloads for ESL/EFL teachers vary according to the setting and whether they have been hired on a full- or part-time basis. It should be said here that because of budget dictates, for the most part, more and more institutions seek to hire part-time teachers when possible. Although this practice helps the institution save money—many part-timers receive no benefits or only partial coverage—it does present problems for teachers wanting and needing to earn a full-time paycheck. In some cases, teachers might be hired full-time but still receive only an hourly wage. What follows is a look at typical workloads and conditions in a variety of settings.

Public Schools

There is a mistaken belief that public school teachers put in a short workday with easy hours, that their day is over when the dismissal bell rings for their students. But, according to the U.S. Department of Labor, Bureau of Labor Statistics, teachers typically work more than forty hours a week when activities outside the classroom are taken into account. Similarly, the Canadian Teachers' Federation reports elementary and secondary teachers average fifty hours a week during the school year and often spend their summers pursuing additional training.

ESL/EFL teachers working in elementary or secondary education within public schools generally follow the same schedule as teachers in other subject areas. A typical day might involve five to six hours of classroom teaching, faculty and parent meetings, involvement in extracurricular activities, supervising lunchtime and recesses, field trips, and a variety of other social and professional events.

Part of a teacher's workload could also involve duties that normally don't fall within the agreed-upon job description. There could be clerical tasks or demands to take over classes for a teacher who is out on sick leave. A double load of students means double the work.

Class size also affects a teacher's workload. An ideal group of twelve students requires less attention than a class of thirty. In a small class there would be less paperwork, fewer exams to grade, fewer problems to deal with, and more individualized progress to achieve.

How students are grouped also affects workload. A class of beginners would require more preparation, patience, and planning than a class of advanced students. A class with students of mixed abilities creates more work than students grouped by the same level of proficiency. Discipline and class-management problems also are factors to consider.

Similar workloads but varying conditions can be expected when teaching primary or secondary education in overseas international schools. These differences are discussed in Chapters 8 and 9.

Postsecondary Education

ESOL instruction in postsecondary education provides training in English to students for use in academic or professional environments. Students may start an ESOL course before beginning their academic program, or they may take both concurrently. Instruction emphasizes language skills, such as reading and writing for academic purposes, and orientation to specific professional/business communities.

There are three main types of programs in postsecondary ESOL.

1. Support system for students entering an academic setting who have been evaluated as needing to improve their proficiency. Their TOEFL scores are low, for example, not meeting the requirements of the institution. Courses range from direct TOEFL preparation to credit-bearing courses in the various language skills. Support programs can be found in college-based language centers or private language institutes.

2. Nonintensive programs offer supervised instruction for at least ten hours a week. Students have some proficiency and concentrate on upgrading one or two particular language skills. Nonintensive programs can be found within an academic department within the university or in separate programs or institutes.

3. Intensive programs entail at least twenty hours of instruction per week. Generally students enrolled in an intensive program need to attain a high degree of proficiency quickly, whether for academic study or professional purposes. The settings for this program are similar to nonintensive programs.

The programs' goals are to achieve the level of English proficiency needed to complete a program of study at the postsecondary level.

In addition to ESL instruction, students are usually provided with cultural orientation, counseling, and academic advising. Facilities that also offer language laboratories, computer-assisted language learning programs, writing/reading labs, and learning or resource centers enhance the program and the students' chances at success.

Adult Education Programs

Community colleges are now a hotbed for ESL education. According to a 2004 study from the Community College Research Center, "The list of community college missions now goes well beyond the core degree granting programs that either lead to transfer or a terminal occupational degree or certificate. Activities now include developmental education, adult basic education, English as a second language . . ."

Adult education programs can be operated from purpose-built centers, on community college campuses, or in public school buildings during evening hours.

Typically, an ESL/EFL teacher hired by an adult education program will work on a part-time basis and be paid an hourly wage.

This wage will compensate the teacher only for the actual number of classroom hours; rarely will it cover time spent in preparation or grading papers and exams.

An adult education teacher working evenings can expect to be assigned between three and fifteen contact hours per week. Class sizes and student levels will vary.

Community Colleges

ESL/EFL teachers working in community colleges within the United States and Canada can be hired part-time and perform under the same conditions as those employed in adult education programs, or they can be hired on a full-time basis. The latter group might teach anywhere from twelve to twenty hours a week, hold office hours, and participate in departmental meetings and related activities.

Hours can be both day and evening, and students will range in age from late teens on up.

Four-Year Colleges and Universities

As mentioned above, teachers can be hired on either a part-time or full-time basis. While part-timers are generally paid an hourly wage, full-time staff benefit from a yearly salary structure. They can be given similar academic rankings as those in other departments—from assistant lecturer/instructor up through assistant, associate, and full professor.

Teachers could be assigned to the university's language center for incoming international students or work in an ESL/EFL program within a specific academic department.

Teaching hours for full-time work range from twelve to twenty periods per week. A part-timer's workload will depend upon the needs of the employer.

Private Language Schools

Conditions vary from school to school but, as in four-year colleges and universities, teachers are employed on a part-time or full-time basis and hourly wage versus yearly salary.

ESL in Bilingual Education

While the only language used in teaching an ESL/EFL class is English, the students' primary languages are vehicles in learning a second language in bilingual education. In a bilingual program, students with the same language background can be grouped together; in an ESL classroom in the United States or Canada, students may come from varied backgrounds.

TESOLers interested in bilingual education teach in classrooms and investigate various issues through research.

Refugee Concerns

Often refugees experience a host of problems trying to assimilate to their new environment while coping with personal losses from a life left behind. Lack of adequate English language skills can exacerbate these problems, adding to feelings of isolation, low self-esteem, and alienation.

ESL teachers working with refugees play an important role in helping to lessen these feelings. Just the act of being assigned to an

ESL class reinforces a sense of self-worth—the student is important enough to be taught.

While not all refugees experience the same level of difficulty, some have so much trouble coping that the stress can contribute to or bring about mental illness. The Refugee Service Center, part of the Center for Applied Linguistics (www.cal.org/rsc), offers materials to help refugee service providers understand the people they're trying to help.

Educational Technology

In a technological society, it is not surprising to find applications for use in educational settings. Computers and the Internet are often used in ESL settings, as well as televisions, overhead projectors, tapes, and cassette recorders. Teachers, for example, might point students to interactive language quizzes or activities available online. There are also extensive resources online for teachers to access lesson plans and other teaching tools. Some of these are listed under Online Teaching Resources in Appendix A. Some teachers even develop online resources students can access from home. But as the Center for Adult English Language Acquisition (CAELA) points out on its website (www.cal.org), "As with any instructional tool, you need to decide what your purposes and goals are first, and then which forms of technology will best serve them."

Videos and DVDs

The use of videos or DVDs in the classroom is widely popular. Teachers work with segments of commercial films or with videos/DVDs designed specifically for use with ESL/EFL instruction. The latter are usually prepared with companion workbooks and teacher's guides. Through the use of videos/DVDs, students can focus on their listening and speaking skills.

Language Laboratory

Another vehicle for helping students with listening skills is the language laboratory. Sometimes in an ESL/EFL program, an instructor will be expected to supervise one or two periods a week in the language lab. This involves learning how to operate the equipment and guiding students through various exercises. It might also involve preparing specific materials for use in the language lab. These labs typically offer computer, audio, and video equipment.

Computer-Assisted Language Learning

Computer-assisted language learning, or CALL, incorporates computers into the language learning process. This can involve software specifically designed for language learners and online learning resources. Several professional journals cover this ever-changing area, including *CALL-EJ Online* (www.tell.is.ritsumei.ac.jp/callej online/index.php), *Language Learning & Technology* (http://llt.msu .edu), and *CALICO Journal* (https://calico.org/p-5-calico%20 jounal.html).

Resource Centers

Resource centers, or learning centers, as they are also called, are generally stocked with TESL/TEFL reading materials geared to different proficiency levels. These may exist within a classroom or in a separate location. Students use their time to improve reading comprehension skills working with textbooks or authentic materials or books adapted for ESL/EFL instruction. Sometimes computers are part of a learning center or a single computer may serve as an individual classroom's learning center.

7

GOING OVERSEAS

TO PREPARE FOR a teaching position overseas, it would be helpful, in addition to the TESOL methodology and theory courses you took in your training program, to study another language and to have some exposure in courses such as international relations, psychology, sociology, and cultural anthropology.

Before you venture overseas, it is also a good idea to have some ESL/EFL experience, paid or volunteer, in a U.S. or Canadian classroom, whether in the public school system, an adult education program, or a university or private language school.

In a U.S. or Canadian ESL classroom, you will most likely meet students from many different cultures. You can talk to your students and learn about their countries. They might also be able to offer you valuable contacts for locating employment overseas.

Finally, seek out other ESL/EFL teachers to ask about their experiences in different countries. Often, the most accurate information you will get is from people who have lived and worked where you want to go.

Who Can Teach Overseas?

Experienced expatriate ESL/EFL teachers are an adventurous breed. As easily as some run down to the corner store, they accept jobs sight unseen in corners of the world they have never traveled to before. They pack up their belongings and spend ten to thirty-six hours on a plane ride, not sure of what they will find when they reach their destination.

Of course, they have done their homework. Throughout the hiring process, they have asked the new employer all the pertinent questions (discussed later in this chapter). Through the TESOL grapevine they have checked out their prospective employer and the working and living conditions of this new setting. They have considered the various accounts and have an idea of what to expect, but they are also aware of how each person has his or her own individual reaction to a place. They are traveling with an open mind, prepared to cope with whatever awaits them.

For a successful stint overseas, keeping an open mind is crucial. The following qualities also are of importance.

• **Flexibility.** Conditions change, and expectations sometimes are not met. Knowing that in advance—expecting that to be the case—will help you adjust.

• **Tolerance.** The concept of tolerance goes by another name as well—*cultural sensitivity*. You have expectations that people from another country might not share. Customs will differ too, and what is acceptable in your country might be offensive in another. It is a good idea to prepare yourself in advance and be willing to adapt your behavior.

• **Patience.** Methods of getting things accomplished will most likely differ from those you are used to. The concept of "I want it yesterday" can suddenly become "Come back tomorrow." The pace in other countries can be much slower and relaxed. After all, what is your rush? You will be there for at least a year or two or more.

• **Independence.** Generally new employers are very helpful in getting their overseas employees settled. Most likely you will be escorted to take care of any initial paperwork—but at some point you will be expected to venture out on your own. A willingness to explore and experience new activities will greatly enhance your stay.

The Hiring Process

Procedures vary from country to country but generally follow a sequence similar to this one: After your application/résumé has been received, you will be contacted for either an in-person interview or by telephone or through the mail for a job offer. You might also exchange a series of e-mails with a potential employer so you can both see if a good fit seems possible. The job offer should be in writing and should state the position for which you are being hired; the exact salary, including allowances and bonuses; housing and other benefits; the length of contract; starting dates; and arrangements for your transportation.

This initial letter will probably request other documentation such as certified copies of your transcripts or diplomas and medical reports. You might be asked to fill out a visa request application and to supply passport information.

You will then be walked through a number of other steps.

Security Checks

Some countries, especially in the Middle East, run a security check on all potential new employees coming to the country. Even after you have been offered your job, find out first if there is a security check and if you have been approved. Before you do anything, such as give notice at your current job, make sure you have been informed, preferably in writing, that you have passed this security check, which often is conducted some time after the job offer.

Passports

You should have your passport ready before you even start applying for jobs. Many job applications require you to fill in your passport information. Visas will be delayed without this. To obtain a passport, you will need your birth certificate or some other proof of citizenship, as well as a valid photo ID. Many post offices keep passport applications on hand. For more specific information, see http://travel.state.gov/passport.

If you already have a passport, make sure it is valid for at least the next six months—and better yet, for the next year. If not, it would be worth your while to renew it before you give your old passport number to your employer. If you change passports after the visa application process has begun, it will have to be started all over again with the new passport information. The delay could take months.

Photos

Once you have been hired, your employer will probably ask you to send a few small photos of yourself and any dependents who will be traveling with you. You will need several more once you arrive, so before you head out, it is a good idea to sit in a photo booth and get a collection of thirty or forty. These will be used for ID cards, residence permits, car insurance, licenses, IDs, and other official documents.

Your Driver's License

If your driver's license is due to expire, it is wise to renew it before you go, and if the date shown on the license is too recent, you should ask the registry of motor vehicles to give you a letter stating how long you have been driving. Some countries will issue you a local license based on a valid U.S. or Canadian license.

Car Insurance

You should also ask the company insuring your automobile to give you a letter stating the number of accident-free years you have accrued. This will help you get a discount on any car insurance you might be purchasing overseas.

Visas

Your employer will most likely arrange your visa for you. Procedures vary from country to country and also change on occasion within each country, but the most common avenues for obtaining visas originate in the host countries or at their U.S. or Canadian embassies.

You might have to take your passport or mail it to the country's embassy to have the visa stamped inside, or the visa can be given to you upon your arrival in the country. Your employer should be able to offer some guidance on how to proceed. Keep in mind that this process can take weeks and even months.

Air Tickets

Your arrival ticket may be arranged by your employer, or you may need to make these travel plans on your own. (Some employers reimburse for these tickets after a specified amount of time.) Online travel sites, such as Travelocity (www.travelocity.com) or Orbitz (www.orbitz.com), are a good way to quickly compare prices from different carriers. If the employer arranges your flight, you will most likely be allowed to choose your own departure date, and you might even be able to arrange a stopover for yourself. It is possible, though, that you won't be able to choose the airline on which you'll be traveling.

Medical Reports

Some employers will request the results of a complete physical, including chest x-ray and an AIDS screening. Be sure to ask about whether you will be reimbursed for this expense.

Before you travel, you should inquire about any potential health hazards and arrange for any immunizations that may be required. The Centers for Disease Control and Prevention offer a broad range of health information for international travelers. You can access information by region or country online at www.cdc.gov/travel. The site also includes a helpful FAQ section and information on what to do before you go overseas.

Other Documents

Some universities and schools require that teachers bring their original diplomas with them. You might have to get them notarized before you arrive. It is also a good idea to have letters verifying the dates of previous employment.

Birth certificates and marriage licenses might also be necessary. The latter might be required to get a visa for your spouse or to collect the financial benefits if you are on married status.

If you are divorced, it's a good idea to carry a copy of that decree with you as well. Your employer might need to see it, and, you never know, you might want to get remarried, and then you would have to produce it.

Remember to pack all important papers in your carry-on luggage. Baggage does go astray, and you will need many of these documents immediately upon arrival.

Questions to Ask

Before accepting a position overseas, there are a number of financial issues you will need to consider. You will want to ask a prospective employer many of the following questions before giving notice on your current job, packing up, and renting out your home. While some ESL/EFL positions are worth the experience alone, most people expect their financial position to improve rather than worsen. These questions may help you determine how the position will affect your finances. You need to ask these questions of both foreign and U.S. or Canadian employers abroad.

Salary
- How will your salary compare to the average salary of a middle-class professional employee in that country?
- Would that professional have to supplement his or her income to maintain a middle-class lifestyle?
- What are the differences in salary/benefits between local and overseas hires?
- Will you be paid in dollars or local currency?
- Is there a free system of currency exchange?
- How often will you be paid? When can you expect your first paycheck?
- Are there bonuses?
- Are there any local income taxes you will have to pay?

- If you are dismissed or the program folds, what guarantees do you have for compensation?
- Will payments be made on your behalf to U.S. Social Security or the Canada Pension Plan?

Personal Possessions
- Will you be reimbursed for storage of your belongings?
- How much weight will you be allowed to ship in and out of the country?
- How much baggage can accompany you in and out of the country?
- Who will pay for shipping and baggage?
- Will you be paid for shipping professional items such as computers and books?

Transportation
- Who pays for your round-trip airfare?
- Will tickets be provided for dependents?
- How often is round-trip transportation offered?
- How will you travel to and from work?

Housing
- Will you be given a choice of housing?
- Who finds accommodations for you?
- Will you be reimbursed for any settling-in expenses?
- If temporary housing is necessary (in a hotel, for example, while waiting for permanent accommodations), who will pay for it?
- Who will pay for deposits, furniture, and household items?
- Who pays for the utilities?
- Will you be able to have a telephone?

Pets
- Are pets allowed where you will be living?
- What medical documentation will you need?
- Is there a quarantine period?
- Who will care for the animal while in quarantine? (Do not assume your pet will be cared for while in quarantine. One U.S. worker in Riyadh, Saudi Arabia, had to travel to the airport twice a day to feed his pet before the authorities finally released it to his care.)

Leave
- How many sick days are you allowed?
- How many vacation days, holidays, and personal and emergency leave days can you expect?

Overtime
- Will you be compensated for substitute teaching?
- If you are required to work beyond the job description (for example, teaching summer sessions), how much will you be paid?
- Are you allowed to engage in outside, part-time employment?

A Word of Caution

Each year, thousands of North American teachers participate in a variety of overseas work-, study-, or travel-abroad programs that are sponsored by private organizations. While the majority of teachers have positive and rewarding experiences in these programs, from time to time, teachers have found that a program was not all it claimed to be.

Because the U.S. government cannot evaluate or recommend specific programs, it has issued guidelines to help you judge a program yourself. Some suggestions for questions to ask are offered here.

The Organization
- What do you know about the organization?
- Is anyone you know familiar with the program?
- Will the organization give you names and addresses of former clients?

Fees
- What will your costs be?
- Are fees itemized?
- Does the organization's literature specify what services are and are not covered?

Refunds
- What provisions have been made for refunds in the event the program is canceled or you change your plans? Read the fine print.

Location of Main Office
- Does the organization have an official base in the United States or Canada—a street address rather than a post office box? It will be difficult to protect or pursue your legal rights in a dispute with a foreign organization unless it maintains some sort of representation in the United States or Canada, subject to those countries' laws.

Underlying Purpose

- Is the organization's main purpose to make work- or study-abroad placements, or does its major interest seem to be in commission-based travel sales?

Orientation

- Advance preparation for the cultural differences should be provided. Some programs provide no orientation or insist upon expensive "required" orientation tours of a week or longer.

Presentation of Program

- Does the organization specify the exact elements of a program's makeup, including duties, pay, lodging, and benefits?

There's also a TEFL School Grey List online (www.esljunction .com/jobs/grey-list-vf5.html) where teachers post descriptions of less-than-perfect experiences with specific schools. A good way to find out about any potential employer is by getting in touch with current or former teachers. There are a variety of websites listed in Appendix A where you can connect with a large community of EFL teachers.

Personal Restrictions

You should be fully aware of any personal restrictions, rules, and regulations before you travel to another country. Forewarned is forearmed. Here is a sampling of some you might encounter.

- **Travel restrictions.** Some countries limit free travel across their borders. Entry and exit visas and permission from your employer or sponsor might be needed to take a weekend away in a neighboring country. It's also a good idea to check the travel warnings issued by the U.S. Department of State (www.travel.state.gov) or the Canadian government (www.voyage.gc.ca/dest/sos/warnings -en.asp). These can alert you to countries where it may not be safe to travel for a variety of reasons.
- **Alcohol.** Some countries, especially some Middle Eastern countries, prohibit the import of alcohol. Although alcohol might be available for consumption once inside the country, there could be stiff penalties for ignoring this restriction. Some countries also prohibit the consumption of alcohol. Most countries have laws banning drinking and driving.
- **DVDs, CDs, books, and other publications.** Many of the Persian Gulf countries in the Middle East are known for their rigorous censorship. Be sure you check with authorities or former teachers before transporting any material that might be considered offensive.
- **Dress.** Conservative countries expect visitors to dress accordingly. While it is not expected that foreigners adopt the national dress, if any, shorts or miniskirts, for example, might offend sensibilities or actually break laws. Again, it is advisable to check this out in advance.
- **Public displays of affection.** Many Persian Gulf countries, for example, are not comfortable with public displays between couples. Be aware of these restrictions for whatever country you are traveling to.
- **Driving.** Saudi Arabia is the only country in which there are restrictions against driving—and these pertain only to women. Women are not allowed to drive under any circumstances in this

country. In exchange, Saudi employers will provide women teachers with transportation to and from work. For personal or social outings, women rely on friends, taxis, or public buses. Restrictions in some parts of the world are a way of life. But restrictions don't mean you won't be able to profit from the experience both professionally and personally.

Personal restrictions are most heavily enforced in the Persian Gulf countries. See Chapter 9 for more about this subject.

Disadvantages

The stress brought about by all of the red tape associated with securing an overseas position, the personal restrictions, and occasional political unrest (if you spend enough time overseas in politically unstable locations, there is a chance that at some point you will run into problems) are some of the disadvantages to an otherwise exciting and fulfilling lifestyle.

Here are a few comments on the subject from some experienced teachers:

> You have to learn to be flexible and tailor what you have to offer to what your employer and the students need. You have to look at the constraints of the particular country. For example, if you love teaching with computers or with slide projectors, be ready to adapt that approach when you move to a country that doesn't have electricity in the classrooms. Sometimes you have to throw your notions or techniques out the window and be very adaptable and sensitive. That is part of the learning you go through.

> Being away from home for long periods of time has its disadvantages. Even though it's very easy to make new friends, it's possible to feel cut off from family and friends at home. You might not be

able to follow local politics or your favorite baseball team, television programs come and go, and all the products with which you're familiar might not be available.

You're very far from your family, and you can feel cut off from world affairs. There's a lot of adjustment you have to go through initially, getting used to a different country. You try not to evaluate what you see until you understand it enough, because it's all so new. When you're living overseas, it's difficult to stay current in the field. Many people stay overseas for a long time, and it's easy to start getting stale. Professionally, the literature is all happening in the United States and Great Britain, and it's difficult to do research or stay professionally active.

Unless you're very dedicated to the language side or you move up professionally into more administrative duties, I don't see it as a profession for life. It's a young people's profession; it can lose its attraction, the longer you do it. After twenty years or so overseas, you can get burned out. To avoid that, it's a good idea to develop an interest in which you can move sideways. Teaching ESL makes you a good communicator, and as a result, you will be good at communicating any other body of knowledge: management training, career and cross-cultural counseling, job skills preparation. I know many ESL teachers who have gone on to become writers or journalists. There are many possibilities.

However, those first few years teaching overseas tend to be very rewarding and very broadening. I feel I have had some wonderful experiences.

In spite of the downsides, many ESL/EFL teachers make working abroad a way of life. Their stays range from one to ten years, or even longer. That, in itself, is proof of how much they are enjoying themselves.

The Real Story

Reputation and the ability to deliver what has been promised are not the only issues to consider when deciding whether to accept a job offer. Concerns about lifestyle, the quality of your accommodations and the standard of living in general, political stability (or the lack thereof), and any personal restrictions are all important considerations. While conducting your investigation, remember that the interviewer might tend to paint an overly rosy picture; a disgruntled former employee might magnify any of the downsides. The real story is probably somewhere in between.

8

OPPORTUNITIES ABROAD

PART OF THE attraction for professionals in the TESOL field is they never know exactly what to expect. You might have done all your research, talked to all the right people, and followed all the advice in the preceding chapters, but when you get on that plane and head off for a new job, you can never be quite sure of what is going to be waiting for you on the other end.

Each country, each city, each employment setting offers something different to each individual who ventures abroad. Successful and content TESOLers are prepared for the unexpected, open to the unpredictable, and view each new job as a gift, a challenge, and an adventure.

Teachers have arrived at their destinations, for example, to find that their entry visas were not in order or that no one had been instructed to meet them at the airport. Their housing was not ready, or their contracts had not been translated into English yet. These problems are not insurmountable and are always worked out eventually—with a little patience and a healthy sense of humor.

On the other hand, teachers have arrived to discover that their standard of living has suddenly skyrocketed beyond what they had expected, that their social life has become a whirl of activity, and that they are using their professional skills to the fullest.

A tolerant attitude will see you through the bumps and allow you to experience all the benefits. But it should be pointed out that some bumps are insurmountable for the individual teacher. Medical facilities could be inadequate, air and noise pollution intolerable, living conditions substandard, working conditions chaotic—all with no hope of improvement. If you have given a place a chance and done what you could to make a situation livable but it still isn't working, there is no shame in packing your bags once again and leaving. This doesn't happen very often, but when it does, an experienced TESOLer knows when it is time to bail out. There is no need to put yourself through a hellish experience; there are slews of other exciting and positive situations to uncover in the world of TESOL. The focus of the rest of this chapter is to help you find those settings.

Who Employs Teachers Overseas?

More and more, education has become an issue of importance around the world. The need for good English-language instruction is a part of that issue. Government agencies; private companies; private and state-funded universities with overseas programs; foreign government branches, such as ministries of education, defense, and information; and foreign private enterprises all have goals that warrant the employment of EFL teachers. Each offers its own set of working and living conditions, salaries, and benefits. What follows is an overview of a variety of settings.

U.S. Government Programs

Stated simply, part of the foreign policy of the U.S. government is to aid developing countries and encourage and support the use of the American educational system overseas. In addition, the U.S. government needs to provide education for dependents of its overseas personnel. With those goals in mind, the U.S. government supports or directly funds a number of programs that regularly hire TESOL professionals.

U.S. State Department American-Sponsored Overseas Schools

The Office of Overseas Schools of the U.S. Department of State provides assistance to independent overseas schools that meet certain criteria. There are two basic purposes for this assistance: to ensure that adequate educational opportunities exist for the dependents of U.S. personnel overseas and to encourage schools that demonstrate American educational philosophy and practice within the countries in which they are located.

Although the relationship between American embassies and various American schools overseas might be close, the schools are all private institutions, responsible for their own staff recruitment. Salary levels and benefits vary from school to school and region to region. Students are generally children of diplomats and others in the international community.

According to a Worldwide Fact Sheet from the U.S. Department of State, "Enrollment in the schools at the beginning of the 2005–6 school year totaled 107,448, of whom 29,045 were U.S. citizens. Of 13,097 teachers and administrators employed in the schools, 5,664 were U.S. citizens." These numbers encompass nearly two hundred schools in 135 countries. A directory of these schools—along with more detailed information—is available at www.state.gov/m/a/os. Or, for more information, write to:

Office of Overseas Schools
Department of State
Washington, DC 20522

U.S. Department of Defense

Elementary and secondary schools have been operating on U.S. military bases overseas since 1946. Children of military and civilian personnel attend these schools. Applications for teachers may be submitted year-round through an online application process; go to www.dodea.edu to find out how. The Department of Defense Dependents Schools (DoDDS) also holds recruiting events in the United States, giving prospective teachers the opportunity to interview. Check the DoDDS website for the latest dates.

Applications must be from U.S. citizens who are available for worldwide posting. ESL teachers must have at least a bachelor's degree or have been certified through a state-approved alternative certification program. Current job openings are listed online, but the department recommends applying by January for positions for the following school year. Overseas employees may be eligible for a living quarters allowance and the shipment of personal goods to the assigned location. Extensive information is available at www.dodea.edu. Or, for more information, write to:

DoDEA Personnel Center
4040 North Fairfax Drive
Arlington, VA 22203

Office of English Language Programs

Within the Bureau of Educational and Cultural Affairs, the Office of English Language Programs puts together a number of educational efforts around the world. These programs are run by the local American embassy or consulate. The office's staff roster includes Regional English Language Officers (RELOs) who work in the United States and overseas. These employees are highly trained TEFL professionals.

According to the U.S. Department of State, "The Office of English Language Programs provides professional teacher training programs worldwide to promote understanding of American language, society, culture, values, and policies. It is only through a thorough understanding of each other's cultures that we can establish and maintain a foundation of international cooperation and trust." General information is available at http://exchanges.state.gov/education/engteaching.

While the office certainly isn't a teacher-placement agency, it does operate two exchange programs of note:

The English Language Fellow Program

This program awards American TEFL professionals ten-month fellowships at educational institutions abroad. One key program goal is to "enhance English teaching capacity overseas in order to provide foreign teachers and students with the communications skills they will need to participate in the global economy." For the 2005–6 school year, the program sent 130 fellows to nearly seventy countries. Applicants must be U.S. citizens and have earned a TEFL/TESL master's degree within the previous seven years. For application information, contact:

Project Manager
English Language Fellow Program
Georgetown University
Center for Intercultural Education and Development
Box 579400
Washington, DC 20057

The English Language (EL) Specialist Program

This program provides TESL/TEFL academics with short stints abroad—typically two to six weeks. These professionals work on specific projects, such as teacher training seminars or English for specific purposes. Applicants must have an advanced degree in TESL/TEFL or applied linguistics, overseas experience, and U.S. citizenship. For additional information, contact:

English Language Specialist Program (ECA/A/L/W)
Department of State (Annex #44)
301 Fourth Street SW, Room 304
Washington, DC 20547

Fulbright Programs

The purpose of the Fulbright Program is to "increase mutual understanding between the people of the United States and the people of other countries. . . ." Grants are awarded to American scholars, students, and teachers to study, teach, and conduct research abroad. Foreign nationals are also funded to engage in similar activities in the United States.

The Fulbright Program includes a range of programs, but three are of most interest to ESL/EFL teachers: the Fulbright English

Teaching Assistantships, the U.S. Scholar Program, and the Fulbright Teacher Exchange Program. For more information on Fulbright programs, visit the program website at http://exchanges.state .gov/education/fulbright. Or write to:

> Office of Academic Exchange Programs
> Bureau of Educational and Cultural Affairs
> U.S. Department of State, SA-44
> 301 Fourth Street SW, Room 234
> Washington, DC 20547

Fulbright English Teaching Assistantships

This program sends grantees to countries around the world to help improve language abilities and general U.S. knowledge at a variety of schools and universities. Applicants must be U.S. citizens and have some knowledge of the language of the host country to which they're applying. Additional details are available at http://us.ful brightonline.org/thinking_teaching.html.

Fulbright Scholar Program

This program funds more than eight hundred scholars and professionals a year in more than 150 different countries. These scholars and other professionals conduct research or lecture in a wide variety of settings and academic and professional fields. More information is available online at www.cies.org/us_scholars.

The Fulbright Teacher Exchange Program

This program creates opportunities not only for college faculty but also for elementary- and secondary-level teachers to trade places with counterparts in countries around the world for a semester or full academic year. In order to be eligible, teachers must already be employed, and they are usually paid the same salary their current position offers.

Candidates must be U.S. citizens, have at least a bachelor's degree, and three years of full-time teaching experience. They also need to be valid U.S. passport holders and fluent in English.

See www.fulbrightexchanges.org for additional information or to complete the online application process. These generally must be received by mid-October to be considered for the following summer or academic year. You can also write for additional details:

Fulbright Teacher Exchange Program
600 Maryland Avenue SW, Suite 320
Washington, DC 20024

Peace Corps

The Peace Corps offers very interesting opportunities for people of all ages, though most new recruits tend to be recent college graduates. Placements are for two-year periods. Remuneration covers training, medical expenses, and transportation. There is no salary as such, but monthly allowances will pay for food, lodging, and incidentals.

EFL volunteers are expected to be qualified in the field. They work in a variety of settings, from rural or traveling classrooms to urban schools or ministries. Their duties range from straight language instruction or training future teachers to curriculum design and consulting.

The training and experience a volunteer receives while in the Peace Corps look impressive on any TESOLer's résumé. Specifics are available at www.peacecorps.gov.

Canadian Government Programs

Canada also has a variety of overseas programs and potential opportunities for ESL teachers. Here are two good places to start:

CANADEM

This clearinghouse is funded by the Department of Foreign Affairs and International Trade. It helps match skilled Canadians with international organizations promoting peace, security, and human rights abroad. The group's website—www.canadem.ca—includes a job postings section, and applicants can apply online for free.

International Youth Internship Program

This government program gives young Canadians the chance to work in a professional capacity abroad. To be eligible, candidates must be between the ages of nineteen and thirty, college graduates, and underemployed or unemployed. Applications and specific international positions are available online at www.acdi-cida.gc.ca/internships.

Universities' Overseas Programs

Many universities and colleges both set up and administer English-language programs with "sister" universities overseas. Funding for these programs comes from a variety of sources, such as state/provincial and federal grants and corporate sponsors, or from the overseas universities themselves. ESL/EFL teachers are usually recruited through advertisements in the *Chronicle of Higher Education* and other publications and at the annual TESOL conference. Salaries are generally competitive, with housing and airfare included.

International Schools

As mentioned previously, the U.S. State Department, through its Office of Overseas Schools, maintains interest in some overseas international schools. Others are independent entities and can be contacted directly for employment possibilities. Addresses for a selected few international schools are supplied in Appendix B. Other addresses can be obtained by contacting the embassy of the country in which you would like to work. Some recruiters for international schools also attend the TESOL conference.

Teachers in international schools are usually paid in local currency. Housing and airfare are sometimes included.

YMCA

The YMCA Overseas Service Corps hires young men and women with TESL/TEFL training or experience for positions overseas. Contact the director at:

OSCY Program
YMCA International Services
6300 Westpark, Suite 600
Houston, TX 77057

Foreign Universities, Colleges, and Technical Schools

Foreign universities, colleges, and technical schools are large employers of EFL teachers. For many overseas institutions, the main language of instruction is English, and language training is necessary to support the academic or technical programs. They may operate entire language centers to cater to the needs of the student population or incorporate an EFL component into the various departments. This is common with many Middle Eastern universities, for example, requiring intensive language training for first-year students.

Other universities might have strong English departments staffed with qualified native speakers. Salaries vary from country to country but are generally competitive and include housing and other benefits.

Universities follow the normal routes for recruitment, including advertising openings in the periodicals mentioned in Appendix A or through agencies and conferences.

Foreign Government Agencies

Some overseas ministries of defense provide English language instruction to their military personnel. Other government departments such as education, information, or health, for example, also hire EFL teachers. Contact appropriate embassies for addresses.

Private Language Schools

Private language centers flourish throughout the world. While many hire teachers locally, others make far-reaching recruitment efforts. Teaching loads can run from twenty to forty hours per week. Housing and airfare may or may not be provided.

Private Companies

Both private companies with overseas operations and foreign private companies often have an ongoing need to provide employees with English language instruction. Time is usually allocated during the employee's workday (common in Japan) to attend classes. In some situations, the employee might be taken off a normal work schedule and enrolled in a training program for one to six months or even longer. Some private companies, such as ARAMCO in Saudi Arabia, also provide schooling for their employees' dependents.

Private companies also advertise in the *Chronicle of Higher Education* or attend recruitment fairs. Salaries and benefits are generally competitive, with housing and transportation provided.

AMIDEAST

This private, nonprofit organization offers English language and professional training to people in the Middle East and North Africa. Teachers can apply for positions in a variety of countries—from Egypt and Jordan to Yemen and Kuwait—working with adults or children. Prospective teachers can fill out applications online at www.amideast.org or contact:

AMIDEAST
1730 M Street NW, Suite 1100
Washington, DC 20036

USAID

Experienced TESOLers often can move into a variety of related positions working with international students at home and abroad. Student counseling, orientation facilitating, immigration, and consulting are just a few of the many areas available.

The U.S. Agency for International Development funds scores of programs worldwide, including education and human resources development. USAID personnel analyze, advise, and assist with the development of host country educational systems. Fellowships and student internships are available, as well as full-time positions. Find out more about career opportunities at www.usaid.gov or contact:

U.S. Agency for International Development
Office of Human Resources
Personnel Operations Division
Room 2.08, RRB
Washington, DC 20523

Going Home

When you first arrive overseas, you are generally helped to settle in, shown around town, taken to the supermarket to stock up your kitchen, and invited to various activities. Soon your social circle begins to widen. Your house or apartment is most likely aleready furnished and paid for. Sometimes utilities are provided as well as transportation.

Your vacation time is extensive; your workload is manageable, perhaps even light. Some days you can go to the beach in the afternoons, out on the town in the evenings, off on exciting treks on the weekends. On your vacations you travel to exotic places you had only dreamed of before. You are making enough money to feel comfortable. After a few years, you can save enough to buy a house back home. You put away your checkbook and credit cards. Finally, perhaps for the first time, you are out of debt.

When it is time to go home, whether by choice or at the end of a nonrenewable contract, giving up that lifestyle is almost as difficult as the initial adjustment was. Many returning expats experience a sort of reverse culture shock. It is difficult to meet new people and get an active social life going. Bills start mounting up—

rent or mortgage payments and telephone calls to your friends still overseas. Out come the credit cards and the checkbook (whose balance is rapidly dwindling).

Jobs at home seem few and far between (that might be why you went overseas in the first place), the salaries might be lower than you have been earning, and now you have to start paying taxes again. Or you might find yourself out of work for a while, ineligible for unemployment benefits. You now have to pay for private health insurance for you and your family.

Returning expats often have difficulty reestablishing credit after long periods away. If you haven't been paying a mortgage or insuring a car in the United States or Canada, it will take some time and patience to qualify for loans or new policies. The best course of action is to try to maintain as much credit activity as is feasible while you are away.

Here is one TESOLer's advice on the subject:

> When you're just starting out, you don't often think of what will happen when it's time to move back home—but there are some real issues to be considered and planned for. It's important to prepare yourself in advance for the time you'll be returning home after several years away. It can be difficult to reestablish yourself. You should maintain your U.S. bank accounts and credit cards, keep renewing your driver's license. And it's a good idea to maintain contact with your university and your professors.

Sometimes the adjustment for the long-term expat is just too difficult. Many come home for a year or so, and then end up back overseas. But for those who really do want to make it work on their home turf, there are some simple ways to help make the transition easier.

When you decide it is time to come home, you will have to give adequate notice, anywhere from 30 to 180 days, depending upon your contract. You can put those last months of waiting time to good use. It is a good idea to go home with a solid plan, and ideally, it is wise to have the assurance of a job waiting for you before you resign your present post. Many are able to accomplish this through all the TESOL contacts they made throughout their stay.

Letting as many people as possible know what you are looking for, writing down as many names and numbers back home as you can accumulate, and getting in touch with these contacts—all this active networking can help have a job lined up and waiting for you upon your return. And if not that, it will give you a head start for when you finally do get home.

Career counselors and other experts will tell you that blindly sending out résumés does little to advance the job search. But if you can touch base with the friend of a friend, he or she might lead you to another friend, and eventually these contacts will pay off. Begin or renew your subscriptions to TESOL professional journals and newsletters and other periodicals mentioned in Appendix A. Some returning expats make a visit home prior to their final departure to start the job hunt. They try to time their arrival to coincide with a TESOL or NAFSA regional or national conference.

Remember to ask for written letters of reference from your employers before you go and perhaps letters of introduction from your colleagues. And don't forget that you are not the same person who went overseas four, five, or ten years ago. You now have acquired many more job skills, including the benefit of your often sought-after international experience. You might have been promoted during your stint—certainly you have matured and ripened. And you now have something more valuable to offer—international experience. You might even find you are in demand.

9

AROUND THE WORLD

WHILE IT IS impossible here to cover working and living conditions for TESOLers in every country of the world, this section looks at selected areas, often through the eyes of teachers who have spent time there.

Learning from Others

Another good source of firsthand information comes from Dave's ESL Café (www.eslcafe.com). This site is a popular online gathering place for teachers. Browse the international job forums, which are divided by country and region, to hear about personal experiences from nearly every corner of the world. There's even a section for teachers getting ready to go abroad for the first time. Post specific questions or simply enjoy connecting and socializing with other professionals.

Thanks to the Internet, there's also a growing number of TEFL bloggers. Teachers often chronicle their experiences while they're actually abroad—giving you an up-close and personal view of what it's like to work in a particular country or even at a particular school. Read about a Canadian's adventures teaching in Hong Kong or the day-to-day life of a teacher in China. TESall.com is currently compiling a teacher blog list at www.tesall.com/bloglist.html. Another option is to browse industry periodicals (see Appendix A). These often include articles written by teachers or featuring their experiences.

Western Europe

There are lots of teaching opportunities in Western Europe at private language schools. Salaries are generally sufficient to cover living expenses, but not necessarily enough to put much away. Housing, transportation, or other perks might or might not be provided depending upon the employer and the country.

Some of the most promising job markets are in Germany, Italy, France, Portugal, and Spain. European Union (EU) passport holders will have a distinct advantage over Americans and Canadians because they can already work legally in any EU country. Those from outside the EU must contend with visas and work permits as part of the job-search process.

Central/Eastern Europe

With the face and philosophies of Central and Eastern Europe changing, teaching English as a foreign language has become of critical importance. In the past, teaching Russian was compulsory and there was little contact with native English speakers. But today, education authorities are making efforts to update and improve their English and other foreign language programs.

There are promising job prospects in a number of countries, including Bulgaria, the Czech Republic, Poland, Romania, and Turkey, for example. Jobs can be found in colleges, universities, and private language schools.

Bulgaria

Bulgaria is located along the western shore of the Black Sea, north of Turkey and Greece, east of Serbia and Montenegro, and south of Romania. In Bulgaria, English is rapidly replacing Russian as the major foreign language. Pay for teachers can be low compared with other countries, but it's typically enough to live on locally. Some teachers supplement their income by giving private lessons on the side. Joyce Adams has worked as a Fulbright scholar in Plovdiv, Bulgaria. "The rooms were poorly heated, dimly lit, and sometimes had no chalk," she wrote in "The Loneliness of the Long-Distance Speakers," an article in *TESOL Matters*. "I used a battery-operated tape recorder I brought from the U.S. The university staff, however, was extremely helpful. Classes were set at an ideal size of twelve, and the students listened respectfully. Americans who go to Bulgaria are well-advised to prepare with extra vitamins for the change in diet and air pollution . . . [but] . . . I recommend teaching in Bulgaria for several reasons. The potential for English language teaching and learning is great, classes are small, and the students are considerably motivated. I realize that Bulgaria is small, but so is a diamond."

Czech Republic

Job opportunities are available at both secondary schools and private language schools, especially in Prague. The pay isn't great, but it's in line with what local workers make. Many teachers supplement their income by teaching private lessons on the side. Overall, the job market for teachers is strong.

Poland

Since Poland joined the European Union in 2004, Americans and Canadians face stiff competition from EU passport holders. Hiring those teachers simply means less paperwork for schools. That said, there are a number of teachers who enjoy working in the country—and it is possible to find work.

Jane Becker taught ESL/EFL in Warsaw on her first assignment overseas with the Peace Corps. Here are some aspects, both negative and positive, of her teaching position: "Classroom interruptions for announcements and use of students as free labor, for example, to build and assemble cupboards, set up election booths with draperies, serve tea to the faculty, wait on tables at faculty parties, lay carpet outside the Deputy Headmaster's office—all at the expense of classes.

But the rewards are the occasional sparks from students who are learning English and their curiosity about American things. I am unable, however, to dispel the notion that all Americans are rich. Thanks to advertising, television, movies, magazines, and the higher quality of all things American, students do not accept the fact that in some instances, very hard work is required."

Romania

After being cut off from the rest of the world for almost fifty years, Romania has been establishing intensive modern language programs and bilingual schools. These programs begin at the elementary school level and continue through junior high, high school, and college. The job market for teachers, however, can be very tough, and pay is often low.

Turkey

Turkey is a delightful country in which to work, although salaries are generally low. But there is a growing EFL marketplace, and jobs for qualified teachers are not too difficult to find.

Asia and the Far East

Some of the best-paying teaching jobs can be found throughout Asia. There's a large demand for teachers in Brunei, China, Japan, South Korea, Malaysia/Singapore, and Taiwan. In fact, some of the highest-paying positions for teachers can be found in these locales.

Brunei

Brunei is a wealthy sultanate with a high standard of living. It is also a Muslim country, so conservative dress is expected. Most teachers are recruited through Great Britain.

China

As China's economy has grown, the market for English teachers has skyrocketed. To help make teaching in China a rewarding experience, it is important to keep an open mind. Things operate quite differently there than in the United States, and this can require an adjustment period. There are opportunities to teach young children through the university level. Jobs are also available with international schools, language schools, and corporations, as well as teaching private lessons.

Students in China are used to lecture-format classes, and it might take them a while to become accustomed to foreign teaching methods that expect class participation. EFL teachers working in China need to be patient, speak slowly at first, and remember to use the blackboard frequently.

Japan

Japan is a fascinating country with a wealth of language-teaching opportunities. ESP is in demand within private industry. Private language schools flourish, and there are many universities.

Japan is also an expensive country, and affordable housing is difficult to find. Most landlords expect up to six months' payment in advance; a large portion of that is considered "key money" and is nonrefundable. Most experienced TESOLers seek out jobs with employers who will provide housing.

Workloads are generally stiff—from twenty-five to thirty contact hours per week. It is possible to enter Japan on a tourist visa to locate employment, but to obtain a work permit, it is necessary to leave the country and reenter with proof of sponsorship from your employer.

JALT, the Japan Association of Language Teachers (http://jalt .org), is a large and active professional group that holds an annual international conference on language learning. Recruiters attend the conference, and it is possible to arrange on-site interviews.

JALT Central Office
Urban Edge Building 5F
1-37-9 Taito, Taito-ku
Tokyo 110-0016
Japan

South Korea

While there is a strong need for English teachers in Korea, many TESOLers report that employers offer little or no support and that teaching materials are either outdated or nonexistent.

Korean employers appreciate visitors to their country who make a strong effort to learn their language. There's also less competition for jobs than in Japan, and most teachers find it quite easy to save money.

John "Ben" Green has been a language instructor for thirty-five years. Of his time in Korea he says, "Seoul, where the majority of TESOLers work, is a very crowded city with huge apartment buildings with hundreds of small apartments. The buses and subways are packed full with no standing room. The best advice I can give EFL teachers is to accept that wherever you are, it's going to be different. For instance, in Seoul, if somebody bumps into you, they won't say, 'Excuse me,' and that's not [considered] impolite. Unless you want to live in a Little America situation, a non-Korean has to say to himself every day, 'I am in Korea, these are their ways, I don't know how they survive, but they are wonderful people . . .' "

Malaysia/Singapore

These two countries take their TEFL teaching seriously. Degrees and certificates are required of all teachers, as are continuing education and professional development. In addition, annual conferences in TESL/TEFL are held to which international as well as local professionals are invited to attend.

The Malaysian English Language Teaching Association (MELTA) publishes a newsletter and provides support to teachers (www .melta.org). Other TESOL-style publications abound.

Taiwan

There's a large demand for English teachers in Taiwan. Pay is generally good, and many teachers report being able to save money. However, some complain about the level of red tape to go through in the country.

The Persian Gulf

Be sure to check with the U.S. Department of State (www.travel.state.gov) or the Canadian government (www.voyage.gc.ca/dest/sos/warnings-en.asp) for current travel warnings. Since the war in Iraq began, a heightened anti-American sentiment has spread through the region. It's also a good idea to read the consular information sheet for any country where you're considering taking a job. These are available online at the same address as the travel warnings. They provide valuable information about a country, including critical points about safety and security.

Since the beginning of the oil boom, hundreds of thousands of Westerners, many of them EFL teachers, have found employment in the Persian Gulf and have enjoyed a high standard of living, a generally safe environment in which to bring up their children, an active social life, and freedom from financial worries.

Because the benefits are so attractive and the "expat" way of life so seductive, most families and singles, originally planning to remain only a year or two for some quick cash, end up staying much longer. Some find themselves staying five years or more.

These oil-rich countries, lacking in the skills necessary for development, are willing and able to provide a comfortable standard of living in return for foreign expertise. For those who are able to adjust to the cultural differences and are willing to sacrifice a little personal freedom (how much depends on the country in which you are working), the positives to life in the Gulf may outweigh the negatives.

When applying for jobs in the Persian Gulf, allow for a long period of red-tape processing. To enter most of the Gulf countries, teachers must be sponsored by their employers, and a variety of government agencies have to communicate with each other to send out job offers, run security checks, and issue visas and work permits. It could take six months to a year from the initial job offer to arrival within the country.

Kuwait

There are positions available for teachers at places like Kuwait University (www.kuniv.edu.kw) and a variety of other schools.

Oman

Oman is a comfortable place for teachers, though it can be somewhat expensive to live there. Alcohol is available, working conditions are usually in modern facilities, and the countryside offers mountains, deserts, oases, and beaches to explore. It is also noted for how clean it is, rivaling Holland and Denmark. It is actually against the law to drive a dirty car in Oman—offenders are regularly stopped and sometimes fined.

Qatar

Qatar is just north of the Emirates, a small Gulf peninsula a little to the south of Bahrain. Alcohol is available in major hotel restaurants and bars and may be purchased by residents. EFL teaching jobs are available, especially in Doha.

Saudi Arabia

Saudi Arabia is a country that can be described with a series of superlatives; it is the largest country on the Arabian Peninsula, the most removed from Western culture, and certainly by far the most restrictive.

It is also a large employer of teachers. In addition to a country-wide system of universities and international schools, private companies such as ARAMCO regularly hire teachers, although many of them have jobs only for men. (In Saudi Arabia, female teachers are allowed to teach only female students.)

Women face the most restrictions in Saudi Arabia. Although they are not expected to don a veil, women must dress extremely conservatively in public. Saudi Arabia is the only country where women are not allowed to drive. It's also important to note that women, especially, can have trouble obtaining an exit visa. Note that both the U.S. Department of State and Foreign Affairs Canada have advised against nonessential travel in Saudi Arabia due to terrorist concerns. Up-to-date information can be found at www .travel.state.gov and www.voyage.gc.ca/dest/sos/warnings-en.asp.

United Arab Emirates

Seven independently governed emirates—Abu Dhabi, Dubai, Sharja, Ajman, Fujaira, Umm Al-Quiwain, and Ra's al Khayma—make up the United Arab Emirates, with Abu Dhabi as the capital.

While Abu Dhabi and Dubai are the most populous emirates, Dubai, about an hour or so away from Abu Dhabi by car, is the most active. It contains tax-free zones and duty-free shopping that attract tourists, both Arabs and expats, from around the Gulf and even farther afield. Life for expats is as comfortable and as varied as it can get, with the usual round of social activities.

Yemen

Although it shares the Arabian Peninsula, Yemen is not one of the oil countries. Jobs do exist there, though there are fewer than in the rest of the Gulf, and salaries and the standard of living are lower. In 2006 the U.S. Department of State issued a travel warning urging U.S. citizens to consider security concerns in Yemen. Up-to-date information can be found at www.travel.state.gov. Foreign Affairs Canada also advised against all travel there due to disputes between the Yemeni government and rebels in the Sa'dah region in the north.

North Africa

North Africa offers a few possibilities for employment but not to the degree of some of the other countries mentioned. Also, there are issues of safety that must be considered.

EFL jobs throughout most of Africa pay so little that the effort to obtain employment there might not be worth it in the end. The Peace Corps and other outreach organizations do have programs there.

Algeria

Algeria has been plagued with political unrest. It is best to check with the U.S. Department of State or Foreign Affairs Canada for current conditions before venturing there. Up-to-date information

can be found at www.travel.state.gov and www.voyage.gc.ca/dest/
sos/warnings-en.asp.

Egypt

While there are a good number of teaching positions available in
Egypt, pay is typically not high, though it is usually enough to live
comfortably in the region. Many teachers enjoy exploring the country's unique history and archaeology firsthand. The Binational Fulbright Commission in Egypt does offer grants to Americans. More
information is available at www.fulbright-egypt.org or by contacting the following:

> The Binational Fulbright Commission in Egypt
> 21 Amer Street
> Messaha, Dokki
> 12311, Giza
> Egypt

Libya

Libya, at this writing, is off-limits for American teachers, but UK
TESOLers find work with oil companies or with the universities
and other schools. Foreign Affairs Canada advises against nonessential travel. Many teachers describe it as a difficult place to live.

Morocco

There are numerous employment opportunities in Morocco. Some
knowledge of French is helpful.

Tunisia

There are not many teaching opportunities in Tunisia, and salaries are generally low. Opportunities are available through AMIDEAST (www.amideast.org).

Other Middle Eastern Countries

The situation in this area of the world is currently very volatile. Anyone considering going there should research his or her options carefully.

Israel

There is some demand for English teachers in Israel. The U.S. State Department and Foreign Affairs Canada issued travel warnings for Israel in 2006. Up-to-date information can be found at www .travel.state.gov and www.voyage.gc.ca/dest/sos/warnings-en.asp.

Jordan

Jordan is traditionally one of the most tolerant and politically stable countries in the Middle East, but the economic situation is poor. Teaching positions are generally available at the university in Amman.

Syria

Proceed with caution, and check with the State Department or Foreign Affairs Canada for current conditions before setting out.

Central and South America

While the region is too large to cover here, it is safe to say that most TESOL employment opportunities are with established organizations and language schools based both in the United States and locally. The rate of inflation is so high in most of these countries that salary figures quickly become out-of-date.

A Word About Etiquette

No matter where you choose to work, you will find customs and habits that differ greatly from those accepted in the United States. Taking time to learn some of the social customs will enhance your stay and help to avoid confusion. Here are a few examples.

• In Turkey, shaking your head doesn't mean "no," it means "I don't understand." Pointing is considered offensive. Raise your eyebrows to signal "no." Conservative clothing is appropriate.

• In India, shaking your head means "Yes, okay, I understand."

• In the Middle East and southern Europe, it is common to see men greet each other with a hug or a kiss on the cheek (both cheeks for special friends). Men also will hold hands with their friends while walking. Women do the same with other women but never with other men. Dress is very conservative, especially for women.

Wherever you are, a willingness to speak the language and understand the culture will always be appreciated.

Appendix A

Job-Hunting and Online Resources

Periodicals

Chronicle of Higher Education
1255 23rd St. NW, Ste. 700
Washington, DC 20037
http://chronicle.com

The *Chronicle* advertises teaching and administrative positions both inside and outside the United States.

EL Gazette
Webscribe, Ltd
P.O. Box 464, Berkhamsted
Hertfordshire HP4 2UR
United Kingdom
www.elgazette.com

The *EL Gazette* newsletter is an e-mail based–publication covering EFL/ESL news, jobs, and events.

English Teaching Forum
ECA/A/L/M
U.S. Department of State, SA 44
301 4th St. SW, Rm. 304
Washington, DC 20547
http://exchanges.state.gov/forum

English Teaching Forum, published by the U.S. Department of State, is a professional quarterly for English teachers around the world.

ESL Magazine
Modern English Publishing
211 E. Ontario St., Ste. 1800
Chicago, IL 60611
or
P.O. Box 50121
32–34 Great Peter St.
London, SW1P 2XD
United Kingdom
www.eslmag.com

ESL Magazine is a bimonthly magazine for ESL/EFL professionals. Select articles online.

Higher Education and National Affairs
American Council on Education
1 Dupont Circle
Washington, DC 20036
www.acenet.edu/am/template.cfm?section=hena

This is the online news resource of the American Council on Education. Free subscriptions are available to "HENA Headlines," which provides twice-weekly e-mail updates.

International Employment Hotline
International Careers
P.O. Box 6729
Charlottesville, VA 22906
www.internationaljobs.org

International Employment Hotline is a monthly newspaper that publishes information on employment, including teaching positions.

International Herald Tribune
6 bis, rue des Graviers
92521 Neuilly Cedex
France
www.iht.com

The *International Herald Tribune* advertises teaching positions in its want-ads section and is available overseas and in some domestic public libraries.

International Living
Agora Ireland
5 Catherine St.
Waterford, Ireland
www.internationalliving.com

International Living is a monthly publication covering working, studying, and living overseas.

Language Magazine
8533 Sunset Blvd., Ste. 202
Los Angeles, CA 90069
www.languagemagazine.com

Access select articles online or subscribe to this monthly magazine.

Network for Living Abroad
P.O. Box 28054
Santa Fe, NM 87592
www.liveabroad.com

Network for Living Abroad is an online publication to help people find resources, contacts, and information about working, studying, and living in other countries. Trade tips on the site's message board or peruse country-specific articles.

OELA Newsline
U.S. Department of Education
Office of English Language Acquisition
400 Maryland Ave. SW
Washington, DC 20202
www.ncela.gwu.edu/newsline

This online news resource provided by the U.S. Department of Education's Office of Language Acquisition includes a job-opportunities section. Free e-mail and RSS (Internet) subscriptions are available.

O-Hayo Sensei
1032 Irving St., PMB 508
San Francisco, CA 94122
www.ohayosensei.com

This is a free electronic magazine on teaching jobs in Japan.

TIE—The International Educator
P.O. Box 513
Cummaquid, MA 02637
www.tieonline.com

The International Educator is a newspaper and interactive website that lists teaching opportunities from around the world.

TES—Times Educational Supplement
Admiral House
66–68 E. Smithfield
London, E1W 1BX
United Kingdom
www.tes.co.uk

The *Times Educational Supplement* advertises ESL/EFL positions all around the world, many of which are not advertised in the United States.

Transitions Abroad
P.O. Box 745
Bennington, VT 05201
www.transitionsabroad.com

Transitions Abroad is a bimonthly magazine covering working, studying, and living overseas.

Books and Directories

The Back Door Guide to Short-Term Job Adventures: Internships, Summer Jobs, Seasonal Work, Volunteer Vacations, and Transitions Abroad, Michael Landes, Ten Speed Press, April 2005.

The Big Guide to Living and Working Overseas, Jean-Marc Hachey, Intercultural Systems/Systèmes interculturels (ISSI) Inc., October 2004.

Chopsticks and French Fries: How and Why to Teach English in South Korea, Samantha D. Amara, Good Cheer Publishing, April 2002.

*Expert Expatriate: Your Guide to Successful Relocation Abroad—
Moving, Living, Thriving,* Melissa Brayer Hess and Patricia
Linderman, Nicholas Brealey Publishing, April 2002.

*The Global Citizen: A Guide to Creating an International Life and
Career,* Elizabeth Kruempelmann, Ten Speed Press, June
2002.

International Exchange Locator: 2005 Edition, A Resource
Directory for Educational and Cultural Exchange, Alliance
for International Educational and Cultural Exchange, 2005.

International Handbook of English Language Teaching, edited by
Christine Davison and Jim Cummins, Springer, October
2006.

ISS Directory of Overseas Schools, International School Services,
2005–2006 edition.

Language Learners in Study Abroad Contexts, edited by Margaret A.
DuFon and Eton Churchill, Multilingual Matters Ltd.,
January 2006.

Opportunities in Teaching Careers, Janet Fine, McGraw-Hill,
March 2005.

Schools Abroad of Interest to Americans, Porter Sargent, October
2006.

Teach Yourself Teaching English as a Foreign/Second Language, David
Riddell, McGraw-Hill, July 2003.

Teaching English Abroad: Teach Your Way Around the World, Susan
Griffith, The Globe Pequot Press, February 2001.

Teaching English as a Foreign or Second Language, Jerry G.
Gebhard, University of Michigan Press, January 2006.

*Teaching English Overseas: A Job Guide for Americans and
Canadians,* Jeff Mohamed, English International, June 2003.

*The World Is a Class: How and Why to Teach English Around the
World,* Caleb Powell, Good Cheer Publishing, April 2002.

Travel Guides

A number of publishers put out in-depth travel guides to various countries and regions in the world. Although not generally a source for jobs, these guides provide important information on living conditions. Check your newsstand or bookstores for appropriate editions. Some popular titles are listed here.

How to Travel Practically Anywhere, Susan Stellin, Houghton Mifflin, April 2006.

Let's Go Southeast Asia, Let's Go Publications, November 2004, www.letsgo.com.

Living Abroad series, Avalon Travel Publishing, www.livingabroadin.com.

Rick Steves' Europe Through the Back Door, Rick Steves, Avalon Travel Publishing, updated annually, www.travelmatters.com.

The Travel Book, Roz Hopkins, Lonely Planet Publications, September 2005, www.lonelyplanet.com.

Online Teaching Resources

General Sites

ESLgo.com
www.eslgo.com

Free lessons plans, activities, and other teacher resources

ESLgold.com
www.eslgold.com

Extensive selection of free materials for teachers

MES English
www.mes-english.com

Free flash cards, handouts, and other resources for working with young learners

Onestopenglish
www.onestopenglish.com

Free classroom resources, teacher forum, and job listings

UsingEnglish.com
www.usingenglish.com

Free handouts, lesson plans, and articles for teachers

Webguides for Teachers
www.webguidesforteachers.com

Round-up site with links to the best resources on technology and teaching

Country-Specific Sites

Ajarn
www.ajarn.com

A comprehensive site on teaching in Thailand

Canadian Association of University Teachers
www.caut.ca

A national organization for academic staff

ELT News
www.eltnews.com

News, resources, jobs, and articles for English teachers in Japan

Expatriate Café
www.expatriatecafe.com

A look at teaching English in Spain

Tealit.com
www.tealit.com

A site for English teachers in Taiwan that includes job and general country information

TESL Canada
www.tesl.ca

A national organization for ESL teachers in Canada

TESOL France
www.tesol-france.org

A nonprofit organization for English teachers in France

Online Job-Hunting Resources

Job Postings and Networking Sites

CareerBuilder.com
www.careerbuilder.com

Comprehensive job site, including ESL teacher postings

Dave's ESL Café
www.eslcafe.com

Online resource and job site for ESL and EFL teachers and students

EducationAmerica.net
www.educationamerica.net

For teaching opportunities across the United States

English Job Maze

www.englishjobmaze.com

For English-teaching jobs around the world

ESL Career

www.eslcareer.com

For teaching jobs across the globe

ESL Jobs

www.esljobs.com

Current employment offerings sorted by regions

ESL Teachers Board

www.eslteachersboard.com

Job listings, school reviews, and résumé section

ESL USA

www.eslusa.org

Job listings, training opportunities, and résumé section

International Employment Gazette

www.intemployment.com

Links useful for international job seekers

Monster

www.monster.com

All-purpose job site with a number of ESL teaching listings

Tefl.com

www.tefl.com

An online professional network for jobs teaching English worldwide

TEFL.net

www.tefl.net

Worldwide listings for EFL jobs, as well as teacher forums and resources

TesAll.com

www.tesall.com

A search portal for accessing ESL/EFL job listings across the Web

Job Placement, Referral, and Information Sources

AFS International Intercultural Programs
71 W. 23rd St., 17th Fl.
New York, NY 10010
www.afs.org

American Association for Adult and Continuing Education
   (AAACE)
10111 Martin Luther King Jr. Hwy., Ste. 200 C
Bowie, MD 20720
www.aaace.org

American Association of Intensive English Programs (AAIEP)
229 N. 33rd St.
Philadelphia, PA 19104
www.aaiep.org

American Educational Research Association (AERA)
1230 17th St. NW
Washington, DC 20036
www.aera.net

AMIDEAST
1730 M St. NW, Ste. 1100
Washington, DC 20036
www.amideast.org

Association for Supervision and Curriculum Development (ASCD)
1703 N. Beauregard St.
Alexandria, VA 22311
www.ascd.org

Center for Applied Linguistics
4646 40th St. NW
Washington, DC 20016
www.cal.org

Educational Career Services
California State University
1250 Bellflower Blvd.
Long Beach, CA 90840
www.ced.csulb.edu/ecs

Educational Research Service (ERS)
2000 Clarendon Blvd.
Arlington, VA 22201
www.ers.org

English International, Inc.
14627 Cypress Valley Dr.
Cypress, TX 77429
www.english-international.com

English UK
56 Buckingham Gate
London, SW1E 6AG
United Kingdom
www.englishuk.com

ERIC Clearing House on Higher Education
1 Dupont Circle NW, Ste. 630
Washington, DC 20036
www.eric.ed.gov

ERIC Education Resources Information Center
c/o Computer Sciences Corporation
4483-A Forbes Blvd.
Lanham, MD 20706
www.eric.ed.gov

Experiment in International Living
Kipling Road, P.O. Box 676
Brattleboro, VT 05302
www.usexperiment.org

Friends of World Teaching
P.O. Box 301994
Escondido, CA 92030
www.fowt.com

Fulbright Scholar Program
Council for International Exchange of Scholars
3007 Tilden St. NW, Ste. 5L
Washington, DC 20008
www.cies.org

Institute of International Education
809 United Nations Plaza
New York, NY 10017
www.iie.org

International School Services
15 Roszel Rd., P.O. Box 5910
Princeton, NJ 08543
www.iss.edu

International YMCA
5 W. 63rd St., 2nd Fl.
New York, NY 10023
www.internationalymca.org

Modern Language Association (MLA)
26 Broadway, Third Fl.
New York, NY 10004.
www.mla.org

National Association for Foreign Student Affairs: Association of
    International Educators (NAFSA)
1307 New York Ave. NW, 8th Fl.
Washington, DC 20005
www.nafsa.org

National Center for Education Statistics
Institute of Education Services
1990 K St. NW
Washington, DC
http://nces.ed.gov

National Clearinghouse for Bilingual Education (NCBE)
The George Washington University
Graduate School of Education and Human Development
2121 K St. NW, Ste. 260
Washington, DC 20037
www.ncela.gwu.edu

National Community Education Association (NCEA)
3929 Old Lee Hwy., #91-A
Fairfax, VA 22030
www.ncea.com

National Council of Teachers of English
1111 Kenyon Rd.
Urbana, IL 61801
www.ncte.org

National Education Association (NEA)
1201 16th St. NW
Washington, DC 20036
www.nea.org

Ohio State University
University Career Services
1945 N. High St.
Columbus, OH 43210
www.careers.ohio-state.edu

Queen's University
Overseas Recruiting Fair
Placement Office
Faculty of Education
Queen's University
Kingston, ON K7L 3N
Canada
http://educ.queensu.ca/placement/index.shtml

School for International Training
P.O. Box 676
Brattleboro, VT 05302
www.sit.edu

Search Associates
P.O. Box 636
Dallas, PA 18612
www.search-associates.com

SIT Professional Development Resource Center
P.O. Box 676
Brattleboro, VT 05302
www.sit.edu/graduate/campus/career.html

Teachers of English to Speakers of Other Languages, Inc. (TESOL)
700 S. Washington St., Ste. 200
Alexandria, VA 22314
www.tesol.org

University Continuing Education Association
One Dupont Circle NW, Ste. 615
Washington, DC 20036
www.ucea.edu

University of Northern Iowa
Overseas Placement Service for Educators
242 Gilchrist Hall
Cedar Falls, IA 50614
www.uni.edu/placemnt/overseas

Worldwide Ministries
100 Witherspoon St.
Louisville, KY 40202
www.pcusa.org/wmd

U.S. Government Agencies

The Defense Language Institute
1759 Lewis Rd., Ste. 142
Presidio of Monterey
Monterey, CA 93944
www.dliflc.edu

The English Language Fellow Program
Georgetown University
Center for Intercultural Education and Development
Box 579400
Washington, DC 20057
http://exchanges.state.gov/education/engteaching/fellows.htm

Fulbright Teacher Exchange Program
600 Maryland Ave. SW, Ste. 320
Washington, DC 20024
www.fulbrightexchanges.org

The Office of English Language Programs
U.S. Department of State (Annex #44)
301 4th St. SW, Rm. 304
Washington, DC 20547
http://exchanges.state.gov/education/engteaching

Office of Overseas Schools
U.S. Department of State
Room H328, SA-1
Washington, DC 20522
www.state.gov/m/a/os

Peace Corps
Paul D. Coverdell Peace Corps Headquarters
1111 20th St. NW
Washington, DC 20526
www.peacecorps.gov

U.S. Agency for International Development (USAID)
Information Center
Ronald Reagan Bldg.
Washington, DC 20523
www.usaid.gov

U.S. Department of Defense
Defense Pentagon
Washington, DC 20301
www.defenselink.mil

U.S. Department of Education
400 Maryland Ave. SW
Washington, DC 20202
www.ed.gov

Selected Employers for ESL/EFL Teachers

These four organizations operate schools throughout the United States and abroad.

Aspect Education
1531 Chapala St., Ste. 1
Santa Barbara, CA 93101
www.aspectworld.com

EF Education First Boston
EF Center Boston
1 Education St.
Cambridge, MA 02141
www.ef.com

ELS Language Centers
Director of Franchise Operations and Curriculum Support
400 Alexander Park
Princeton, NJ 08540
www.els.edu

Inlingua International
Belpstrasse 11
3007 Bern
Switzerland
www.inlingua.com

Other Resources

EFL-LAW.org
www.efl-law.org

A blog on legal and other TEFL issues

TEFL Blacklist
http://teflblacklist.blogspot.com

Teachers share unsavory experiences

Appendix B

Job Contacts by Country

MANY COUNTRIES RECRUIT teaching staff through their embassies. When writing or calling a specific country's embassy, contact the education office or cultural affairs office. You can also write to a specific country's ministry of education; the address is available through the embassy.

Africa

Cote d'Ivoire

International Community School of Abidjan
c/o U.S. Embassy, Abidjan
Department of State
Washington, DC 20521
www.icsa.ac.ci

Egypt

The American University in Cairo
113 Kasr El Aini St.
P.O. Box 2511
Cairo, 11511
Egypt
www.aucegypt.edu

The Binational Fulbright Commission in Egypt
21 Amer St., Messaha
Dokki, 12311, Giza
Egypt
www.fulbright-egypt.org

Cairo American College
P.O. Box 39
Maadi 11431
Cairo, Egypt
www.cacegypt.org

Kenya

Association of International Schools in Africa
c/o International School of Kenya
P.O. Box 14103
Nairobi 00800, Kenya
www.aisa.or.ke

International School of Kenya
P.O. Box 14103
Nairobi 00800, Kenya
www.isk.ac.ke

World Relief
7 E. Baltimore St.
Baltimore, MD 21202
www.wr.org

Morocco

Casablanca American School
Route de la Mecque,
Lotissement Ougoug,
Quartier Californie,
20150 Casablanca
Morocco
www.cas.ac.ma

Asia

East Asia Regional Council of Overseas Schools
Brentville Subdivision, Barangay Mamplasan
Biñan, Laguna, 4024
Philippines
www.earcos.org

China

Association of Commonwealth Universities
36 Gordon Sq.
London WC1H OPS
United Kingdom
www.acu.ac.uk

China Teaching Program
MS-9047
Western Washington University
516 High St.
Bellingham, WA 98225
www.ac.wwu.edu/~ctp

CIEE, Teach in China
7 Custom House St., Third Fl.
Portland, ME 04101
http://ciee.org

City University of Hong Kong
Tat Chee Ave.
Kowloon, Hong Kong
www.cityu.edu.hk

Education Office
Embassy of the People's Republic of China
2300 Connecticut Ave. NW
Washington, DC 20008
www.china-embassy.org
or
515 St. Patrick St.
Ottawa, ON K1N 5H3
Canada
www.chinaembassycanada.org

International School of Beijing
No. 10 An Hua St.
Shunyi District, Beijing 101300
The People's Republic of China
www.isb.bj.edu.cn

Voluntary Service Overseas
317 Putney Bridge Rd.
London, SW15 2PN
United Kingdom
www.vso.org.uk

Indochina

ACG International School
Jl. Warung Jati Barat No.19
Ragunan, South Jakarta
Jakarta, 12510
Indonesia
www.acgedu.com

Fund for Reconciliation & Development
355 W. 39th St.
New York, NY 10018
www.ffrd.org

School for International Training
Kipling Rd., P.O. Box 676
Brattleboro, VT 05302
www.sit.edu

Voluntary Service Overseas
317 Putney Bridge Rd.
London, SW15 2PN
United Kingdom
www.vso.org.uk

Japan

AEON Corporation
1960 E. Grand Ave., Ste. 550
El Segundo, CA 90245
www.aeonet.com

Berlitz Schools of Languages in Japan
JS Kariya-eki Bldg. 1F 1-24
Sakuramachi
Kariya-City 448-0028
Japan
www.berlitz.com

JALT: The Japan Association of Language Teachers
Urban Edge Bldg. 5F
1-37-9 Taito, Taito-ku
Tokyo 110-0016
Japan
http://jalt.org

The Japan Exchange and Teaching Program
Embassy of Japan
Office of JET Program
2520 Massachusetts Ave. NW
Washington, DC 20008
or
255 Sussex Dr.
Ottawa, ON K1N 9E6
Canada
www.mofa.go.jp/j_info/visit/jet

Osaka YMCA International Program
1-2-2-800 Benten Minato-ku
Osaka 552-0007
Japan
www.oyis.org

Tokyo Center for Language and Culture
1-20-1 Shibuya, Sanshin Bldg. 6
Shibuya-ku, Tokyo 150-0002
Japan
http://tclc-web.co.jp

Philippines

Cebu Pacific International Language School
M.J. Cuenco Ave.
Cebu City
Philippines
www.cpils.com

Harvest Christian School International
24-B Tres Borces St.
Mabolo, Cebu City
Philippines
www.hcsinternational.org

South Korea

Dong-A University
840 Hadan2-dong
Saha-gu, Busan 604-714
Korea
http://english.donga.ac.kr

Korea International School
155 Gaepo-dong
Kangnam-gu, Seoul
Korea
www.kis.or.kr

Pagoda
1306-6, 7 Seocho-Dong
Seocho-Gu, Seoul, 137-855
Korea
www.jobpagoda.com

Singapore

National University of Singapore
21 Lower Kent Ridge Rd.
Singapore 119077
www.nus.edu.sg

Taiwan

YMCA of the USA, International Division
101 N. Wacker Dr.
Chicago, IL 60606
www.ymca.net

Thailand

Ruamrudee International School
6 Ramkhamhaeng 184
Minburi, Bangkok 10510
Thailand
www1.rism.ac.th

Volunteer Service Overseas
317 Putney Bridge Rd.
London, SW15 2PN
United Kingdom
www.vso.org.uk

Central and South America

Association of American Schools of Central America
Colombia-Caribbean and Mexico
c/o U.S. Embassy Quito
Unit 5372, Box 004
APO AA 34039-3420
Quito, Ecuador
www.tri-association.org

Association of American Schools in South America
14750 NW 77th Ct., Ste. 210
Miami Lakes, FL 33016
www.aassa.com

Inter-Regional Center for Curriculum and Materials Development
Apartado Aereo 3250
Barranquilla, Colombia

Brazil

American School of Brasilia
Avenido L-2 Sul
SGAS 605, Bloco E, Lotes 34/37
70200-650 Brasilia, DF
Brazil
www.eabdf.br

Chile

Comunicorp
Hernando de Aguirre 129
Providencia, Santiago
Chile
www.comunicorp.cl

Colombia

Centro Colombo Americano
Director, English Programs
Cra. 45 (El Palo) No. 53
24 A. A. 8734 Medellin
Columbia
www.colomboworld.com

Europe and Russia

Central and Eastern European Schools Association
Vocarska 106
Zagreb 10000
Croatia
www.ceesa.org

European Council of International Schools
21B Lavant St., Petersfield
Hampshire, GU32 3EL
United Kingdom
www.ecis.org

(For schools in Western Europe)

Mediterranean Association of International Schools
c/o American School of Madrid
Apartado 80
28080 Madrid
Spain
www.mais-web.org

(For schools in Spain, Portugal, France, Morocco, and Tunisia)

Bulgaria

Anglo-American School of Sofia
DOS/Management Officer
5740 Sofia Pl.
Washington, DC 20521

Czech Republic

Next Level Language Institute
Pohorelec 147/8
118 00 Prague
Czech Republic
www.nextlevellanguage.com

Denmark

Copenhagen International Junior School
Hellerupvej 22-26
2900 Hellerup
Denmark
www.cis-edu.dk

France

International School of Paris
6 Rue Beethoven
75016 Paris
France
www.isparis.edu

Germany

The Language Lounge
Desmond Dawson
Holtorfer St. 15
53229 Bonn
Germany
http://thelanguagelounge.de

Greece

Infolingua
Educational Center of Foreign Languages and Computers
32 Baknana, Athens
Greece
www.infolingua.gr

Hungary

International Further Studies Institute
6000 Kecskemet
Petofi S. u. 2. III/5
Hungary
www.ifsi.hu

Poland

British Council Poland
Warsaw Centre
Al. Jerozolimskie 59
00-697 Warsaw
Poland
www.britishcouncil.org/poland

Russia

BCK-IH Moscow
15 Starovagankovsky Pereulok
Office No. 3
121019 Moscow
Russia
www.bkc.ru

Spain

Ben Franklin International School
Martorell i Peña, 9 08017
Barcelona
Spain
www.bfis.org

English International College
Urb. Ricmar
Crtr. de Cádiz—Málaga Km. 189,5
Marbella, Málaga
Spain
www.eic.edu

Middle East

Most universities in the Middle East, especially in the Persian Gulf
countries, operate a language center for incoming students. Unless
otherwise specified, your letter of application can be sent to the language center director.

Near East South Asia Council for Overseas Schools
c/o The American Colleges of Greece
Gravias 6
Aghia, Paraskevi 15342
Athens, Greece
www.nesacenter.org

Israel

Jewish Agency for Israel
633 Third Ave., 21st Fl.
New York, NY 10017
www.jewishagency.org

Kuwait

American University of Kuwait
P.O. Box 3323
Safat 13034
Kuwait
www.auk.edu

Embassy of the State of Kuwait
2940 Tilden St. NW
Washington, DC 20008
or

333 Sussex
Ottawa, ON KIN 1J9
Canada

Oman

The American-British Academy
P.O. Box 372, PC 115
Medinat Al Sultan Qaboos, Muscat
Sultanate of Oman
www.abaoman.edu.om

Embassy of the Sultanate of Oman
2535 Belmont Rd. NW
Washington, DC 20008

Sultan Qaboos University
P.O. Box 50
Muscat 123
Sultanate of Oman
www.squ.edu.om

Qatar

Academic Staff Recruitment Committee
University of Qatar
P.O. Box 2713
Doha, Qatar
www.qu.edu.qa

Embassy of the State of Qatar
2555 M St. NW
Washington, DC 20037
www.qatarembassy.net

Saudi Arabia

There are numerous colleges, universities, and technical and vocational schools as well as international schools throughout Saudi Arabia. Private companies also are frequent hirers of teachers. Private companies that advertise their openings can be located in directories of overseas businesses. Here are some starting points.

American International School—Riyadh
P.O. Box 990
Riyadh, 11421
Kingdom of Saudi Arabia
www.aisr.org

The Institute of Public Administration
Recruiting Office
English Language Center, IPA
P.O. Box 205
Riyadh 11141
Saudi Arabia
www.ipa.edu.sa

King Abdulaziz University
P.O. Box 1450
Jeddah 21441, Saudi Arabia
www.kaau.edu.sa

King Fahd University of Petroleum Minerals
Dhahran 31261
Saudi Arabia
www.kfupm.edu.sa

King Saud University
College of Arts
P.O. Box 2454
Riyadh, 11451
Saudi Arabia
www.ksu.edu.sa/english

Raytheon International Support Company
Raytheon Company
870 Winter St.
Waltham, MA 02451
www.raytheon.com

Royal Embassy of Saudi Arabia
601 New Hampshire Ave. NW
Washington DC 20037
www.saudiembassy.net
or
99 Bank St., Ste. 901
Ottawa, ON K1P 6B9
Canada

Saudi Aramco
P.O. Box 5000
Dhahran 31311
Saudi Arabia
www.saudiaramco.com

Syria

Damascus Community School
Al Mahdi Bin Baraka St.
Abu Rumaneh, Damascus
Syria

Department of State
6110 Damascus Place—DCS
Dulles, VA 20189-6110
www.dcssyria-db.org

International Center for Agricultural Research in the
    Dry Areas (ICARDA)
P.O. Box 5466, Aleppo
Syrian Arab Republic
www.icarda.org

United Arab Emirates

Embassy of the United Arab Emirates
3522 International Ct. NW, Ste. 400
Washington DC 20008
http://uae-embassy.org
or
45 O'Connor St., Ste. 1800
World Exchange Plaza
Ottawa, ON K1P–1A4
Canada

Higher Colleges of Technology
Recruitment Department
P.O. Box 47025
Abu Dhabi
United Arab Emirates
www.hct.ac.ae

The United Arab Emirates University, Al Ain
P.O. Box 15551, Al-Ain
United Arab Emirates
www.uaeu.ac.ae

Yemen

Arabic in Yemen
P.O. Box 11727
Sana'a, Yemen
www.arabicinyemen.com

Sana'a International School
Box 2002
Sana'a, Yemen
http://yem.qsi.org

U.S. Territories

American Samoa

Department of Education American Samoa
Pago Pago, American Samoa 96799
www.doe.as

Commonwealth of the Northern Mariana Islands

Department of Education
CNMI Public School System
P.O. Box 501370
Saipan, MP 96950
www.pss.cnmi.mp

Guam

Guam Public School System
Attn: Personnel Services Division
P.O. Box DE
Hagåtña, Guam 96932
www.gdoe.net

Puerto Rico

Department of Education
P.O. Box 190759
San Juan, PR 00919
www.gobierno.pr

U.S. Virgin Islands

Department of Education
No. 44-46 Kongens Gade
Charlotte Amalie
U.S. Virgin Islands 00802
www.usvi.org/education

Teacher Training Programs

Reference Books

Directory of Teacher Education Programs in TESOL in the United States and Canada, 2005–2007, edited by Virginia Christopher, published by TESOL. Information on more than four hundred programs in the United States and Canada.

Professional Development for Language Teachers: Strategies for Teacher Learning, Jack C. Richards and Thomas S. C. Farrell, published by Cambridge University Press, April 2005.

Intensive Short-Term Training Courses

Australia

ACL
157–161 Gloucester St.
The Rocks
Sydney NSW 200
Australia
www.acl.edu.au

International House Sydney
Teacher Training & Professional Centre
Level 3, 89 York St.
Sydney NSW 2000
Australia
www.training.ihsydney.com

Canada

Canadian College of Teachers
90 Dundas St. West
Mississauga, Ontario L5B 2T5
Canada
www.collegeofeducators.ca

Greystone College Vancouver
342 Water St., 2nd Fl.
Vancouver BC V6B 1B6
Canada
www.greystonecollege.com

Sprott-Shaw International Language College
340 Victoria St., 3rd Fl.
Kamloops, BC, V2C 2A5
Canada
www.ssilc.com

Egypt

The American University of Cairo
113 Kasr El Aini St.
P.O. Box 2511
Cairo, 11511
Egypt
www.aucegypt.edu

France

The American University of Paris
6, rue du Colonel Combes
75007 Paris
France
www.aup.fr

Greece

British Council Greece
17 Kolonaki Sq.
106 73 Athens
Greece
www.britishcouncil.org

CELT Athens
77 Academias St.
106 78 Athens
Greece
www.celt.edu.gr

Japan

Teachers College
Columbia University
Mitsui Seimei Bldg. 4F
2-21-2 Misaki-cho
Chiyoda-ku, Tokyo 101-0061
Japan
www.tc-japan.edu

Temple University, Japan Campus
2-8-12 Minami Azabu
Minato-ku, Tokyo 106-0047
Japan
www.tuj.ac.jp

Philippines

De La Salle University–Manila
2401 Taft Ave.
1004 Manila
Philippines
www.dlsu.edu.ph

Spain

International House Barcelona
c/o Trafalgar 14
08010, Barcelona,
Spain
www.ihspain.com

Switzerland

Erziehungsdirektion des Kantons Bern
Sulgeneckstrasse 70
3005 Bern
Switzerland
www.erz.be.ch

Volkshochschule des Kantons Zurich
Sekretariat VHS
Splügenstrasse 10
CH-8002 Zürich
Switzerland
www.vhszh.ch

United Kingdom

Bell International
Hillscross
Red Cross Lane
Cambridge CB2 2QX
England
www.bell-centres.com

Hilderstone College
Broadstairs
Kent CT10 2JW
England
www.hilderstone.ac.uk

i-to-i TEFL Courses UK
Woodside House
261 Low La.
Leeds LS18 5NY
United Kingdom
www.teflcourses.com

International House
16 Stukeley St.
Covent Garden
London WC2B
England
www.ihlondon.com

Pilgrims English Language Courses
4–6 Orange St.
Canterbury, Kent
CT1 2JA
United Kingdom
www.pilgrims.co.uk

Regent Brighton
18 Cromwell Rd.
Hove, BN3 3EW
United Kingdom
www.regent.org.uk

Regent Cambridge
119 Mill Road
Cambridge, CB1 2AZ
United Kingdom
www.regent.org.uk

Regent Edinburgh
29 Chester St.
Edinburgh, EH3 7EN
United Kingdom
www.regent.org.uk

Regent London
12 Buckingham St.
London WC2N 6DF
United Kingdom
www.regent.org.uk

Regent Margate
Northdown House, Margate
Kent, CT9 3TP
United Kingdom
www.regent.org.uk

Regent Oxford
90 Banbury Road
Oxford, OX2 6JT
United Kingdom
www.regent.org.uk

SKOLA Teacher Training
SKOLA English in London
27 Delancey St.
London NW1 7RX
England
www.skola.co.uk

St. Giles Brighton
3 Marlborough Pl.
Brighton
Sussex BNI IUB
United Kingdom
www.stgiles.co.uk

St. Giles Eastbourne
13 Silverdale Rd.
Eastbourne
Sussex BN2O 7AJ
United Kingdom
www.stgiles.co.uk

St. Giles London Central
154 Southampton Row
London WC1B 5JX
United Kingdom
www.stgiles.co.uk

St. Giles London Highgate
51 Shepherds Hill
Highgate
London N6 5QP
United Kingdom
www.stgiles.co.uk

TEFL International
60 N. Road East
Plymouth
Devon
PL4 6AL
United Kingdom
www.teflinternational.org.uk

United States

These schools offer the Cambridge CELTA (Certificate in Teaching English to Speakers of Other Languages), which qualifies teachers for TESL/TEFL work in many foreign countries.

Bridge Linguatec Inc.
915 S. Colorado Blvd.
Denver, CO 80246
www.bridgelinguatec.com

Cy-Fair College
9191 Barker Cypress Rd.
Cypress, TX 77433
www.cyfaircollege.com

Intercultural Communications College
1601 Kapiolani Blvd., #1000
Honolulu, HI 96814
www.icchawaii.edu

International House Portland
155 B Avenue #220
Lake Oswego, OR 97034
www.ih-usa.com

International House San Diego
2725 Congress St. Suite #2M
San Diego, CA 92110
www.ih-usa.com

International House Santa Monica
530 Wilshire Blvd., Ste. 105
Santa Monica, CA 90401
www.ih-usa.com

North Harris College
2700 W.W. Thorne Dr.
Houston, TX 77073
http://celta.nhceducatesu.com

St. Giles International San Francisco
One Hallidie Plaza, Ste. 350
San Francisco, CA 94102
www.stgiles-usa.com

About the Author

Blythe Camenson began her career as an ESL/EFL teacher at a private language school in Florida. From there, she accepted an overseas job at King Saud University in Riyadh, Saudi Arabia, the beginning of an eight-year stint that included positions in a private language school in Kuwait, a four-year term as a university instructor in Oman, and her last overseas job as director of courses with the American Cultural Center (USIS) in Baghdad. Camenson evacuated in August 1990, nine days after the Iraqi invasion of Kuwait. She rode in the first convoy of evacuees from the U.S. embassy to the Jordanian border.

As a full-time writer of career books, Camenson works hard to help job seekers make educated choices. She firmly believes that with enough information, readers can find long-term, satisfying careers. Toward that end, she researches traditional as well as unusual occupations, talking to a variety of professionals about what their jobs are really like. In all of her books, she includes firsthand accounts from people who can reveal what to expect in each occupation.

Camenson earned her B.A. in English and psychology from the University of Massachusetts and her M.Ed. in counseling from Northeastern University. She has written more than two dozen books for McGraw-Hill.